Iraq at the Crossroads: State and Society in the Shadow of Regime Change

Edited by
Toby Dodge and
Steven Simon

Adelphi Paper 354

Oxford University Press, Great Clarendon Street, Oxford OX2 6DP
Oxford New York
Athens Auckland Bangkok Bombay Calcutta Cape Town
Dar es Salaam Delhi Florence Hong Kong Istanbul Karachi
Kuala Lumpur Madras Madrid Melbourne Mexico City
Nairobi Paris Singapore Taipei Tokyo Toronto
and associated companies in
Berlin Ibadan

Oxford is a trade mark of Oxford University Press

Published in the United States
by Oxford University Press Inc., New York

First published January 2003 by **Oxford University Press** for
The International Institute for Strategic Studies
Arundel House, 13–15 Arundel Street, Temple Place, London WC2R 3DX
www.iiss.org

Director John Chipman
Editor Mats R. Berdal
Design Manager Simon Nevitt

British Library Cataloguing in Publication Data
Data available

Library of Congress Cataloguing in Publication Data

ISBN 0-19-852837-X
ISSN 0567-932x

Contents

Biographies

Amatzia Baram

Dr Amatzia Baram is a professor of Middle East History at the University of Haifa, Israel. He was awarded his PhD in 1986 by the Hebrew University of Jerusalem, and has been teaching at Haifa since 1982. In the 1990s, Dr Baram spent a year as Senior Associate Member at St Antony's College, Oxford, a year as Fellow at the Woodrow Wilson International Center for Scholars in Washington DC and a year with the US Institute of Peace, also in Washington DC. He has been studying Iraqi history, politics, society and culture since the late 1970s. He has published two books and numerous articles in professional magazines.

Toby Dodge

Dr Toby Dodge is a Research Fellow at the ESRC Centre for the Study of Globalisation and Regionalisation, University of Warwick, where he is working on the transformation of the Middle East and the wider developing world under globalisation. He has recently published *Globalisation and the Middle East; Islam, Economics, Society and Politics*, co-edited with Professor Richard Higgott (London and Washington: Royal Institute of International Affairs and the Brookings Institution, 2002). Before joining Warwick University he worked with the Middle East Programme at The Royal Institute of International Affairs. His research there focused on the use of coercive diplomacy in the post-Cold War world and the transformation of Iraq under economic embargo and war. A book,

Iraq under sanctions: violence, poverty and war will be published by Blackwells in early 2003. Research for the book was carried out in Iraq over the past two years. Toby last visited Baghdad in September 2002. Before working at RIIA he completed a PhD on the transformation of the international system in the aftermath of the First World War and the creation of the Iraqi state at the School of Oriental and African Studies, University of London. He also taught international relations and Middle Eastern politics in the Department of Political Studies at SOAS for four years.

Faleh A. Jabar

Dr Faleh A. Jabar is an Iraqi sociologist, based in London. He holds a PhD in Political sociology (Birkbeck College, University of London), and he is research fellow at Birkbeck. His recent publications include: *State and Civil Society in Iraq* (Cairo: Ibn Khaldun Centre, 1995); *Post-Marxism and the Middle East* (London: Saqi Books, 1998); *Ayatollahs Sufis and Idoelogues* (London: Saqi Books 2002); *Tribes and Power in the Middle East* (London: Saqi Books, 2002). His, *The Shia Movement in Iraq* is to be published in February 2003.

Isam al Khafaji

Dr Isam al Khafaji, BSc, MA, Doctorat de Trosisieme Cycle Economics, Summa Cum Laude PhD Social Sciences, is an Iraqi writer and scholar. Born in Baghdad in 1950, he lives now in the Netherlands, where he teaches on state and nation formation and consolidation, globalisation and development at the International School of Humanities and Social Sciences at the University of Amsterdam. He is also a consultant with the World Bank, Washington DC. Last year, he was a senior expert for the United Nations Development programme for the preparation of Syria's first national human development report. Before that he was a visiting professor at New York University. He has lectured and participated in conferences at several universities including Harvard, Princeton and Georgetown. Al Khafaji is the author of three books in Arabic and numerous papers and articles in Arabic, English, Dutch, German and Persian on theoretical issues as well as on the politics, economics and society in the Middle East in general and Iraq in particular. Al Khafaji has edited and sat on the editorial boards of several reviews and periodicals including the *Middle East Report*, of which he is a contributing editor.

Michiel Leezenberg

Michiel Leezenberg is assistant professor in the Faculty of Humanities at the University of Amsterdam. His main research interests are the Kurds, Islamic intellectual traditions, and the foundations of the human sciences. He made several research trips to Iraqi Kurdistan, and has published extensively on politics, society and economics of the region. In 2001 he published *Islamic Philosophy: A History* (in Dutch), which was awarded the prize for the best Dutch-language philosophy book of the year.

David Ochmanek

David Ochmanek is a senior analyst at RAND. He has held several positions in the United States government, including service in the United States Air Force, the Department of State and the Department of Defense, where he was Deputy Assistant Secretary of Defense for Strategy from 1993 to 1995. His most recent book is *The Real and the Ideal: Essays on International Relations in Honor of Richard H. Ullman*, co-edited with Anthony Lake (Lanham, MD: Rowman & Littlefield, 2001).

Steven Simon

Steven Simon is Assistant Director of the International Institute for Strategic Studies and Carol Deane Senior Fellow in American Security Studies. Before joining IISS in November 1999, he served on the National Security Council staff at the White House for five years, concentrating on Persian Gulf security strategy and counter-terrorism. Prior to his White House assignment, he held a succession of posts at the Department of State, including Director for Political-Military Plans and Policy and Acting Deputy Assistant Secretary of State for Regional Security Affairs. Mr Simon appears regularly on London-based media outlets (TV, web, radio) to discuss US-European relations, American politics, and Middle Eastern affairs and has been published by *TIME*, the *New York Times*, *Washington Post*, *Wall Street Journal Europe*, *Asian Wall Street Journal*, *Financial Times*, *International Herald Tribune*, *Christian Science Monitor*, *Strategic Survey*, the *New York Review of Books* and *The New Republic*, as well as scholarly journals, including *Survival*, *World Politics*, and *Politique Internationale*. He has advanced degrees from Harvard and Princeton and held fellowships at Brown University and Oxford University.

He is co-author of *The Age of Sacred Terror* (New York: Random House, 2002).

Gareth Stansfield

Dr Gareth Stansfield is a Leverhulme Special Research Fellow in the Institute of Arab & Islamic Studies at the University of Exeter. He lived in Iraqi Kurdistan between 1997 and 2001 working in Arbil and Suleimaniyah alongside the Kurdistan Regional Government(s). His PhD was completed at the University of Durham and addressed the political development of the *de facto* Iraqi Kurdish state. It is soon to be published as *Iraqi Kurdistan: Political Development and Emergent Democracy*. His current research focuses on the future political development of Iraq, addressing the possibilities for its domestic economic and political rehabilitation and reintegration into the international community.

Judith S. Yaphe

Dr Yaphe is a Senior Research Fellow in the Institute for National Strategic Studies (INSS) at the National Defense University, Washington DC. She specialises in Iraq, Iran, and the Arabian/Persian Gulf. Before joining INSS in 1995, Dr Yaphe was a senior political analyst for the US government and received the Intelligence Medal of Commendation for her work on Iraq and the Gulf War. Her publications include articles on 'U.S. Policy Towards Iraq', *RUSI International Security Review* (December 1999); 'Iraq: Human Rights in the Republic of Fear', *Human Rights and Governance in the Middle East, 1998*); 'Do No Harm: Arab perspectives on NATO's Mediterranean Initiative', *The Mediterranean Quarterly* (November 1999); 'Some Thoughts on Tribalism in Iraq', *Middle East Policy* (June 2000); and 'Iraq: The Exception to the Rule', *The Washington Quarterly* (Winter 2000). She is co-author of *Strategic Implications of a Nuclear-Armed Iran* (Fort McNair DC: NDU Press, 2001) and author of *The Middle East in 2015: the Impact of Regional Trends on U.S. Strategic Planning* (Fort McNair DC: NDU Press, 2002). She received a BA with Honours in History from Moravian College and a PhD in Middle Eastern History from the University of Illinois.

Introduction

On 19 December 2002, Hans Blix, the Chairman of UNMOVIC (the UN inspections authority for Iraq) declared to the UN Security Council that Iraq's 12,000 page declaration of its weapons of mass destruction programme (WMD), submitted as required by UNSC Resolution 1441, was incomplete and had significant gaps. Any further impediment placed before the inspectors would be enough to constitute 'material breach' of the Resolution and would lead to the overthrow of the regime. The invasion, occupation and potential political reconstitution of Iraq will have profound implications not only for the Iraqi people, but for neighbouring countries as well. Depending on how the United States and its allies formulate their war objectives, how quickly resistance collapses, and how deep the West's commitment and stamina proves to be in the post-war era, Iraq's population could find itself under a replica of the current regime or on an extended trajectory towards liberalisation and perhaps even eventual democracy.

It can be argued that renewed war with Iraq was inevitable. Sooner or later, the intertwined pressures of domestic Iraqi politics, Saddam Hussein's self-image as leader of the Arab world, his pursuit of WMD, Iraqi anti-Zionism and the regime's tendency to misapprehend the international environment were going to bring Baghdad into a decisive confrontation with the United States.[1] The timing of this confrontation was determined by an event wholly outside the control of the two main protagonists, Iraq and the United States, yet intimately related to the first phase of their rivalry: the emergence of a global *jihad* movement dedicated to the destruction of Islam's presumed adversaries. It was the 1991 Gulf War that galvanised this movement, provided its animating imagery and refocused *jihadist* wrath away from Arab governments on to the 'far enemy', a favoured euphemism for the United States. The Gulf War also revivified a popular Islamic eschatological literature that had surged after the Six Day War of 1967, in which apocalyptic dreams of the destruction of New York City were a staple feature.[2] The successful attempt by al-Qaeda to transform this dream of the night into the reality of the day on 11 September 2001 catapulted Iraq to the top of a new American administration's agenda and put Baghdad and Washington on a collision course.

US Iraq policy before 11 September

The Clinton administration had expressly favoured regime change, but regarded the cost as prohibitive. Veterans of the first Bush administration who formed George W. Bush's foreign and defence policy advisory team during his presidential campaign and now constitute his national security cabinet had argued throughout the 1990s that the American declaratory position on regime change should be forcefully implemented. Leaving aside the normative issues that regime change raised, the Bush team assessments of the Clinton administration's commitments to removing Saddam by force was correct. For Clinton's team, the disincentives were considerable. The Iraqi opposition was feckless and disconnected from events on the ground. Basing countries were unenthusiastic, European allies uncooperative. Other priorities such as the Middle East peace process and the Balkans crisis were too pressing, economic uncertainties too great, and the military options too unappetising to both the Joint Chiefs of Staff and the civilians in the White House and Pentagon to risk a major military engagement. Moreover, sanctions enforcement, although clearly weakening, was far from disintegrating. The Clinton administration could plausibly argue that the UN escrow scheme and the oil-for-food programme effectively deprived Saddam of the resources needed to reconstitute his military strength, while reducing the adverse effect of sanctions on the lives of ordinary Iraqis. Saddam, as administration spokespersons routinely stressed, was 'in the box'.

These arguments were challenged not only by Republicans, but also by powerful Democratic critics, including Senator Joseph

Lieberman of Connecticut, who would become the candidate for the vice-presidency in 2000. The Iraq Liberation Act (HR 4655) was championed by a bipartisan coalition in Congress, but signed reluctantly by President Clinton in October 1998 only after extensive wrangling over its scope and funding. The Iraqi opposition that was so appealing to its friends in Congress was far less persuasive at the White House, or at the Central Intelligence Agency (CIA), which was saddled with the responsibility of undermining the Iraqi regime through covert action. In the wake of the debacle of 1996, in which the CIA infrastructure in northern Iraq was dismantled in an Iraqi incursion that the US military was powerless to prevent, the CIA was not overly eager to start again. Accordingly, despite significant political pressure from both sides of the congressional aisle and Iraq's increasing non-cooperation with UN Special Commission weapons inspectors in 1998 and their eventual withdrawal, the Clinton team put Iraq on the back burner after the large-scale *Operation Desert Fox* air strikes of December 1998, which Republican critics derisively dubbed 'the pinprick'.

Once in office, however, the Bush administration continued its predecessor's approach.[3] The new team had higher priorities than forcing regime change in Iraq. The testing and deployment of large-scale missile defences, which would require American withdrawal from the Antiballistic Missile (ABM) Treaty of 1972, threatened to reprise the intra-Atlantic Alliance crisis of the mid-1980s over the deployment of nuclear-tipped intermediate range ballistic and cruise missiles in Europe. US-Russian relations were entering a delicate phase and no one could be confident that Moscow would acquiesce in Washington's stated intention to scrap the decaying strategic architecture of the Cold War and transcend its reliance on mutual assured destruction. China was branded a strategic competitor by the administration, which quickly became embroiled in a succession of small crises involving, *inter alia*, a presidential pledge to do whatever was necessary to defend Taiwan against Chinese aggression and a subsequent collision off the Chinese coast between a US spy plane and a Chinese tactical aircraft. Although the administration successfully withdrew from the ABM Treaty while keeping relations with Russia on track and stabilised relations with China, the intensive diplomacy required to reach these objectives crowded out efforts to move forward towards regime change.

In keeping with its perception that the world had changed in a way that demanded a new strategic paradigm, the White House and civilian Pentagon leadership embarked on an audacious restructuring of entrenched military planning, programming and budgeting practices. Given the apparent absence of immediate adversaries and the emergence of rapid technological advances on which the US seemed to have a monopoly, the new team saw an opportunity to skip a generation of weapons and take a fresh look at the missions and structure of American forces. The uniformed services opposed these initiatives, however, and precipitated a crisis that was widely thought to presage the resignation of Secretary of Defense Donald Rumsfeld and his cadre of reform-minded appointees.[4] At home, the White House was focused on an exhaustive study of American energy options, based on a stated belief that a crisis was looming, and on lobbying for a large, multi-year tax cut in an economy that was edging towards recession. With its hands so full, there would be scant opportunity or motivation to put Republican campaign rhetoric on Iraq into action.

Philosophically as well as pragmatically, there was no urgent interest in the Middle East among foreign-policy managers who believed that American interests were bound up with the actions of other major powers, rather than small countries on the periphery of world affairs. From the new administration's perspective, key alliances – particularly NATO and treaty ties to Korea and Japan – had been neglected and there had been a failure to focus on potential adversaries, such as China and Russia, which truly had the capacity to challenge American interests in the future. Other countries, with the possible exception of India, were marginal to a worldview that was self-defined as disciplined, realistic, and disinclined to see foreign policy as social work.[5] The Palestinian–Israeli front was not seen as ripe for intervention, while the main Persian Gulf player, Saudi Arabia, was perceived as unreliable and potentially hostile. Indeed, the administration's determination to diversify domestic and foreign energy sources was not unrelated to its distrust of Saudi Arabia and scepticism about the long-term prospects of its rulers.

The effect of 11 September

The attacks of 11 September did not completely overturn the administration's existing priorities or invalidate its early instincts.

Nevertheless, the sudden, shocking apprehension of the vulnerability of the United States to a devastating attack on its territory made it hard not to think about other adversaries who might have the will and ability to hit Americans in the same way. Al-Qaeda's objective was to cause mass casualties. Looking at the carnage in lower Manhattan – especially in aerial photographs – Americans could not help but think that New York looked as though it had been hit with a nuclear weapon. The terrorists were known to be flirting with WMD, a fact confirmed by evidence recovered from Taliban and al-Qaeda installations in Afghanistan. The scale and brutality of the attacks suggested that if al-Qaeda had possessed a nuclear device on 11 September, it would have used it. The anthrax attacks that followed (and remain unsolved) reinforced the burgeoning public perception of the threat posed by WMD.

Administration officials and a small number of influential outside advisors grasped the opportunity to raise the profile of Iraq by intimating that Saddam Hussein was linked to one or another of these attacks. Although the Kurdish opposition has argued that the regime in Baghdad had worked with Ansar al-Islam and Jund al-Islam, two *jihadist* groups in northern Iraq that had connections with al-Qaeda, a review of the intelligence failed to turn up specific information showing that Saddam was complicit in either attack.[6] Reports that Muhammad Atta, the ringleader of the group that carried out the 11 September operations, had met with the chief Iraqi intelligence officer in Prague were unconvincingly documented by the Czech intelligence service and ultimately repudiated by the Czech government. Convinced that the CIA was withholding relevant reports on contacts between Iraq and al-Qaeda, the Pentagon created its own intelligence cell where state-of-the-art data-mining software is being used to re-examine all-source reporting on this issue.[7]

The absence of a smoking gun has not mattered, however, because decision-makers and the public have concentrated not on the question of Saddam Hussein's culpability for 11 September, but on the possibility that Iraq might at some point transfer WMD materials or components to al-Qaeda or a similarly motivated non-state group. Iraq's enormous stocks of anthrax in this context were like the proverbial elephant in the living room. They could not be ignored, despite the lack of evidence that Iraq had been directly involved in terrorism against the US. The point was, rather, that Iraq was a place where terrorists could obtain WMD. To be sure, the vast ideological gap between the secular Ba'athist regime in Baghdad and the *salafist* orientation of the terrorists, as well as Saddam's obsession with control over his WMD assets, suggested that transfer of such materials would be unlikely. But the bulk of informed opinion coalesced not around probabilities, but consequences.[8] Thus, cooperation between al-Qaeda and Iraq on WMD might be unlikely, but if it took place, the risk to America's populations would be unacceptably grave. As President Bush's national security advisor phrased the problem, the United States could not afford for the smoking gun to be a mushroom cloud.

Within the administration, these developments coincided with – and helped to shape – an ongoing process of strategic reinvention. The unwillingness to rely exclusively on deterrence that had underwritten the administration's commitment to ballistic missile defence was leading US planners to explore the other strategic option in a world where deterrence was no longer deemed credible: pre-emption. What these thinkers really meant was something more preventive than pre-emptive, inasmuch as they were contemplating the need to deprive an adversary of a dangerous capability well before any crisis had materialised in which it might actually be brought to bear. In the flow of post-11 September events, Iraq naturally emerged as the first candidate for preventive attack. Decision-makers who had seen 47 senators vote against US military intervention in Kuwait in 1991 for fear of high casualties asked how the Senate would vote in a future contingency involving war against a nuclear-armed Iraq. Would America be deterred from defending its interests in such a situation? Analysts conceded that Saddam could be deterred – he had, after all, refrained from using WMD in the Gulf War – but feared that his tendency to misjudge his adversaries would result in his future disregard for American threats of retaliation. It was not so much that deterrence no longer worked, but that Saddam might not 'get it'.[9]

A slow march

Despite the momentum developing towards war, an administration decision to forge ahead was not forthcoming. In early 2002, proponents of robust regime change had made considerable progress but had not yet won the day. The president made clear that military operations in Iraq would have to await the stabilisation of the situation in Afghanistan. Military planners endorsed this step-by-step approach, asserting that the US was already overstretched, munitions stocks were low and intelligence collection platforms were over-committed. The State Department also favoured a go-slow approach to gain time for the difficult diplomacy that war preparations would entail. Against a backdrop of Palestinian–Israeli violence, for which the US was (and is still is) judged responsible by many in the region, the State Department would have to win basing, access and overflight rights from an array of countries; foster a semblance of unity among disparate opposition groups; and prepare the ground at the UN and in capitals for a possible presidential decision to attack Iraq.

Nearly two years after the Bush administration took office and over a year after the 11 September attacks, war has not yet broken out.[10] The president's decision to seek a UN Security Council resolution was foreordained, although Secretary of State Colin Powell used his influence skilfully to bring the drama to a close by persuading the president that such a decision would work to Washington's advantage by short-circuiting brewing opposition both at home and abroad. Public opinion polls were clear about American willingness to support a war within the framework of UN authorisation and their corresponding reluctance to approve unilateral military action. Indeed, US and European attitudes tend to converge on this point.[11] If the P-3 fail to achieve consensus in New York, whenever it is that the US and UK return to the Security Council under the terms of the deal that resulted in UNSCR 1441, it will be because the Anglo–American entente judges gaps in Iraq's declaration that are borne out by the United Nations Monitoring and Verification Commission (UNMOVIC) to be evidence of continuing material breach and therefore *casus belli*, while the French, followed by the Russians and Chinese, interpret such a development as a sign that inspections are working and war is unnecessary.

Having gone to New York, the US will have to live with the consequences. Secretary of Defense Rumsfield and Vice-President Dick Cheney are on record as dismissing the utility of inspections on the not-unreasonable basis that the regime's ability to conceal its holdings is better than the UNMOVIC's capacity to reveal them.

These high-level policymakers reflect a widely held suspicion, in the UK as well as the US, that inspections might result in a clean bill of health for a Saddam who nevertheless continues to hold stocks of WMD. They therefore conclude that the regime must go. In contrast, President Bush, whose political future would depend on the outcome of a war, has stated consistently that the issue is disarmament. His remark to the effect that a regime decision to disarm would constitute regime change was not entirely ironic.

Should Saddam miscalculate, either out of the conviction that the US intends to unseat him regardless of his efforts to cooperate with inspections, or because he thinks he can drive a wedge within the Security Council by adopting a posture of ambiguous cooperation and a propaganda campaign aimed at publics in surrounding countries, war will be inescapable. The regime's past behaviour suggests that such miscalculation is more likely than not. Indeed, the absence in Iraq's declaration of any attempt to account for sizeable stocks of prohibited material may have made war inescapable.[12] Hence this book. A major land war in the heart of the Middle East, aimed at the elimination of a 34-year regime and undertaken in the context of a global *jihad* against the US and its allies will have unforeseeable effects on the interests of the combatants themselves and the region as a whole. These effects will be influenced, if not determined, by the course of the war – who resists and for how long? – and modalities of occupation – whom do the conquerors recognise? Governments that have little knowledge of the evolution of Iraqi state and society over the past three decades are prone to costly and enduring mistakes. We hope that the insights offered by the panel of distinguished contributors will minimise this risk.

The papers were originally prepared for a one-day workshop entitled 'Iraqi Futures' held at the International Institute for Strategic Studies in October 2002. We deliberately avoided any attempt to impose on these essays a unitary editorial voice since our intention was to bring to the public debate the diversity of informed opinion on the key issues.

Judith Yaphe, a former CIA analyst and now professor at the National Defense University, opens the *Adelphi Paper* by parsing the roots of Washington's push for a resolution of the 11-year stand-off between Iraq and the UN ceasefire demand for disarmament. She identifies and defines the major impulses at work, clarifies their institutional links and posits a comprehensive list of questions that war (and post-war) planners in the US and presumably in other countries that support intervention diplomatically or militarily must answer. In the next essay, David Ochmanek, a former Clinton administration senior defence official (now at the RAND Corporation), who was influential in shaping the Pentagon's war plans in the 1990s, sets the stage by describing the strategy and forces that the US would use in a war with Iraq. Although he does not touch on the likely British contribution (a reinforced armoured brigade), or a possible French contingent – both of which would be subordinated to American command and incorporated into the Pentagon's plan – Ochmanek makes clear that the invasion force will be large and will fight in Baghdad if Saddam forces that outcome by retaining control of the cities. Neither reliance on advanced technology nor the appeal of the 'Afghan model' of special forces fighting alongside indigenous militias will obviate the need for a robust invasion force. Saddam's troops are unlikely to crack unless faced with an overwhelming adversary and post-war order cannot be sustained by a handful of special forces.

Toby Dodge (Centre for the Study of Globalisation and Regionalisation, University of Warwick) used his research on the transformation of the Iraqi state under sanctions and several recent trips to Iraq to provide an overview of how key Iraqi institutions will react to a large-scale assault. He looks carefully at how the Ba'ath leadership has successfully maintained its control over the army and internal security services in the face of an eight-year war with Iran, the massive defeat of 1991 and the uprisings in the south and north of the country that followed. The regime has sacrificed the military efficiency of the Iraqi armed forces to ensure they do not pose a threat to Saddam Hussein's continued rule. This means that although conventional military opposition to an invasion may be shortlived, a coup launched against the regime from within the security services will happen, if at all, in the final moments of any war. The military campaign will be fought in the cities of Iraq, primarily Baghdad, against a background of intense international media coverage.

Isam al Khafaji (International School of Humanities and Social Sciences, University of Amsterdam) a leading scholar of Iraqi politics and economics questions the 'primordialising' of Iraq prevalent in current policy prescriptions, the conventional wisdom that stresses the heterogeneity of society with its supposed ancient ethnic and religious divides. He goes on to argue that the Ba'ath Party since 1968 have largely managed to atomise Iraqi society, making individuals directly dependent on state largesse. The contemporary growth of tribalism in Iraq is best understood as a regime tactic to strengthen its rule in the face of sanctions. Khafaji uses his knowledge of the evolution of Iraq, the Iraqi opposition in exile and US policy to passionately argue against post-regime change solutions that are either externally imposed or dependent upon militias organised around political parties.

It is a cliché that Saddam's Iraq is governed by a 'Tikriti mafia'. Amatzia Baram, (Professor of Middle Eastern History at Haifa University) applies his encyclopaedic knowledge of Iraq to demonstrate in detail how Tikritis are distributed throughout the top ranks of the army, security services and party, delineates their tribal connections and speculates how the presence of this Tikriti and tribal network is likely to shape the regime's resistance to a US-led attempt to topple Saddam.

Faleh Jaber (Birckbeck College, University of London) has deployed his long career as a sociologist of Iraq and extensive research in the north of Iraq earlier this year to scrutinise how the army has evolved over the last 20 years and how it may react to a military campaign against it. Saddam Hussein has managed to successfully inject networks of clan and kinship into the army, giving him a freer hand in its supervision and control. However, Jabar strongly argues against any comparison with the recent military campaign against the Taliban in Afghanistan. In the face of a military assault, the army may react in ways comparable to 1991 with sections opting for mutiny, some surrendering and yet others retaining their cohesion and fighting to defend the government. Jabar concludes that a coup is unlikely unless the US succeeds in attracting a considerable segment of the ruling tribal alliance to their side.

Gareth Stansfield (Institute of Arab and Islamic Studies, University of Exeter) considers the plight of the four million Kurds that live in the enclave that gained *de facto* autonomy from Baghdad in the aftermath of the 1991 revolts. Since then, this enclave has seen economic growth, but also the intervention of regional powers, political instability and a bitter civil war between the two main political parties, the Kurdistan Democratic Party (KDP) and the Patriotic Union of Kurdistan (PUK). Today it is threatened by political uncertainty in the shadow of regime change. Both the KDP and PUK face the potential for political marginalisation as a new government is installed in Baghdad and their political and economic autonomy is placed in doubt. For Michiel Leezenberg (Department of Philosophy, University of Amsterdam) Iraq Kurdistan has made important political and economic strides even if these do not amount to real pluralism or economic liberalism. But the durability of these gains is open to questions. Leezenberg points to massive emigration, an increase in intra-societal and domestic violence, and the failure of Kurdish authorities to maintain social services that neither Baghdad nor NGOs provide. These failings have provided the classic opportunity for increased Islamist activity, which could be an impediment to a stable post-war Kurdistan. Nevertheless, he argues for a cautious optimism: media freedom; the presence of competing parties rather than a single small elite; and the integration of Kurdistan into the oil economy suggests the possibility of a brighter future for northern Iraq.

Faleh Jabar in a second contribution to this volume analyses the social organisations that exist in the south of Iraq and that may, potentially, take part in any popular uprising to overthrow the Ba'athist regime. He makes the point that the Shia community in Iraq is not a monolithic bloc. The picture in the south of the country is much more complex. After crossing into Iraq from Iran in 1991, the exiled Shia organisations – the Supreme Council for the Islamic Revolution in Iraq and the Dawa Party – found that they were unable to lead the rebellion sparked by Iraq's defeat in the Gulf War. These organisation's close association with Iran and their use of overtly religious imagery alienated the rebellious soldiers retreating from Kuwait and other secular-minded or non-sectarian rebels. Jabar argues that the regime's post-war suppression of southern society resulted in the growth of religious networks and charitable services. It is from these indigenous organisations that any potential opposition leadership will arise during regime change.

This book and the workshop it sprung from required a huge effort to bring to light. We are especially grateful to Ahmad Lutfi of the IISS Middle East programme and James Green, Manager for Editorial Services, for their cheerful cooperation under intense pressure. We were also given crucial help by the *Survival* editorial team, Dana Allin and Jill Dobson, and by Jonathan Stevenson, the editor of the IISS *Strategic Survey*. Their intelligence, collegiality and resilience make the IISS the great institution it is.

Toby Dodge
Steven Simon
London and Washington
December 2002

Notes

[1] On domestic politics, see Charles Tripp, *A History of Iraq* (Cambridge: Cambridge University Press, 2nd ed., 2002). On Iraq's quest for weapons of mass destruction, see *Iraq's Weapons of Mass Destruction: A Net Assessment*, IISS Strategic Dossier, International Institute for Strategic Studies, 9 September 2002.

[2] See Daniel Benjamin and Steven Simon, *The Age of Sacred Terror* (New York: Random House, 2002).

[3] For the administration's initial approach to Iraq see Toby Dodge, 'Iraq: Smart Sanctions and Beyond', *The World Today*, (Vol. 57, No. 3, June 2001).

[4] This problem is ongoing. See Vernon Loeb and Thomas E. Ricks, 'Rumsfield style, goals, strain ties in Pentagon', *Washington Post*, 16 October 2002. p. A01.

[5] This phrase was used by Michael Mandelbaum to capture a tendency in Clinton foreign policy that the author believed had vitiated American power; it became a mobilising slogan for advocates of a less sentimental approach. See Michael Mandelbaum, 'Foreign Policy as Social Work', *Foreign Affairs*, vol. 75, no. 1, January/February 1996, pp. 16–32.

[6] See 'Al-Qaeda in Northern Iraq? the elusive Ansar al-Islam', *Strategic Comments*, Vol. 8, Issue 7, Sept. 2002 IISS.

[7] See Eric Schmitt, Thom Shanker, 'Threats and Responses: a CIA Rival; Pentagon sets up Intelligence Unit', *The New York Times*, p.A1

[8] The argument against the proposition that Saddam would transfer weapons or materials to al-Qaeda is summarised in Daniel Benjamin, 'Saddam Hussein and Al Qaeda Are Not Allies', *New York Times*, 30 September 2002, p. A25. Sceptics also noted that the greatest danger of WMD use by Saddam would be in a regime change scenario, and the greatest likelihood of transfer to al-Qaeda would be in the fog of war.

[9] A powerful case for this has been made by Kenneth Pollack, *The Threatening Storm: The case for Invading Iraq* (New York: Random House, 2002).

[10] Although as of this date, the forces needed to begin military operations are already in place. See Eric Schmitt, 'Buildup Leaves U.S. Nearly Set to Start Attack', *New York Times*, 8 December 2002, p. A1.

[11] For a detailed comparison of U.S. and European views on the conditions under which an attack on Iraq would be justifiable, see Philip H. Gordon, *Iraq: The Transatlantic Debate*, Occasional Paper No. 39, Paris: European Union Institute for Security Studies, December 2002.

[12] David E. Sanger and Julia Perston, 'Iraq Arms Report has big omissions, US official say', *New York Times*, 13 December 2002, p. A1.

Chapter 1

America's War on Iraq: Myths and Opportunities

Judith S. Yaphe

During the summer of 2001, conservative supporters of the Bush administration were still finding their places at the table in the Vice-President's Office, the Pentagon, the State Department, and on the little known and much maligned Defense Policy Board, an advisory group comprised of former government officials from the winning side and the conservative think-tanks that helped plot the election victory. They made clear their strong support for Israel in its war with the Palestinians and their advocacy of regime change in Iraq and Iran. Until September 2001, not much attention was given to their quest to remove Saddam Hussein. Much critical attention, however, was paid to the Bush administration's reluctance to involve itself in the violence that marked the destruction of the peace process begun under the administration of the George H.W. Bush.

This changed with the events of 11 September. After the terrorist attacks on the Twin Towers in New York City, the Pentagon, and the aborted attack in Pennsylvania, the neo-conservative foreign and defence policy advisers to George W. Bush were catapulted to prominence. Dubbed the neocons by their critics, they espoused the global war on terrorism, which they soon designated by 'phases' – Phase 1: Get Osama bin Laden, destroy al-Qaeda, and eliminate

Afghanistan as a safe haven and launching point for terrorists to attack the United States, its allies and friends; Phase 2: get Saddam Hussein, destroy his Ba'athist regime and establish democratic government in the New Iraq. Some even argued for a Phase 3, in which the state sponsors of terrorism from the present and past – Syria, Iran, Libya, parts of Lebanon, Colombia, even China – would be purged of their evil, unrepresentative, non-elected regimes and brought into the new world of democratic enlightenment.

This paper will examine the debate and the debaters on what policy the United States should pursue regarding Iraq, and consider some of the myths and realities, risks and opportunities that our policy choices represent. This is not intended to be an examination of the second Bush administration's Middle East policy as a whole nor of its efforts – or lack thereof – in trying to resolve tensions between Israelis and Palestinians. The focus here is Iraq.

Washington's myths and myth-makers

As have all administrations, the Bush administration has been inundated with advice from the right and ultra-right wings of the Republican Party, as well as from the Democrats and the remnants or descendants of 1960s liberal-left elements. While the neocons of the Republican Party are the dominant influence on foreign and defence policy-making,[1] all of the groups offering advice have a constituency either in the government, the press, the think-tanks, and/or the private sector. The following list gives a flavour of who is advising what on Iraq to whom:

The truth as released by the administration: In this version, current in the Office of the Vice-President, the National Security Council, the Office of the Secretary of Defense and elements in the State Department and the halls of Congress, Saddam is evil. He is responsible for the death and destruction of Iraq as well as wreaking havoc on neighbouring Iran and Kuwait. He used chemical weapons on his own people and on Iranians during their 8-year war in the 1980s. He has allowed war, economic sanctions imposed by the UN, and a cruel government-controlled system of wage and price controls and monopolies, to reward friends and family while destroying Iraq's once-burgeoning middle class and making all Iraqis more dependent on him for their well-being. He sponsors international terrorist groups, giving them training, safe haven, weapons and operational assistance, although Baghdad still cannot be linked to al-Qaeda directly and the events of 11 September. He is determined to retain and rebuild the weapons of mass destruction (WMD) programmes banned by UN Security Council Resolution 687, particularly nuclear and biological weapons. He will never accede to disarmament by any UN body, be it UNSCOM or its light version, UNMOVIC.[2] If the US is present in the Gulf to protect its access to the region's energy resources – gas and oil – then he represents a threat to that interest, as well as to neighbours who have allowed the US access to their military facilities to maintain monitoring flights under *Operation Northern Watch* (out of Turkey) and *Operation Southern Watch* (from Saudi Arabia and Kuwait). Saddam is a danger to Iraqis, to the neighbourhood, to Israel and, existentially, to us. The only solution is regime change and its replacement by a democratically installed government. Vice-President Cheney is in the forefront of those calling for a pre-emptive attack on Iraq.[3]

The truth as divined by the Neocons: Conservative think-tanks such as the American Enterprise Institute, its director Richard Perle, and the former director for Central Intelligence James Woolsey expand on the above scenario. They view Iraq as the 'strategic prize' and are enthusiastic supporters of Ahmed Chalabi and the Iraqi National Congress. Once liberated, they say, Iraq will provide the spark to transform the region – the Palestinians, Iran, Syria, Saudi Arabia, and ultimately even Egypt – from autocracy to democracy. The New Iraq will make peace with Israel and join with us as a strategic partner against Iran, the real threat in the region. Few US forces will be needed. Instead, we can apply the lessons learnt from the war on terrorism in Afghanistan – smart bombs, air power, special forces, and an ally on the ground. No coalition will be necessary – we can do this with only Turkey, Kuwait and the UK, of course, to help us. As these conservatives are fond of saying, 'Determination breeds success'. If we attack, we will be successful, and 'they' will follow. Others call for a more 'muscular' response to Saddam in order to prevent the region from becoming a 'chaotic platform for greater global terrorism'. One prominent editorial writer noted in June that the US needs to rely more on a greatly expanded and intrusive military presence in the region to support diplomacy. 'American forces,' he said, 'would stay for years to help develop and shield new and democratic leaderships in Iraq and in a Palestinian state.'[4]

The truth as designated by the Military: For the Joint Chiefs and the Combatant Commander of US Central Command, General Tommy Franks, the picture is more complicated and risky. We can do it, they say, but don't ask us now with your plans and under your conditions. Even under the Clinton administration, military plans called for 200,000 to 300,000 ground forces in addition to air power and the new generation of smart weapons. Different strategies are being discussed. Should it be a war with few US troops and Iraqi 'allies'? Should it be a multi-prong attack or an inside strategy focused on taking Baghdad? I leave this discussion more appropriately to military analysts.[5]

The truth as determined by the New (or Old) Left: In contrast to the neocons, the neoleft depicts war as immoral and war against Iraq as illegal. It will only punish the Iraqi people; they rarely mention the regime or Saddam. Members of groups such as Voices in the Wilderness and the Education for Peace in Iraq Center (EPIC), which do charitable good works, also naïvely believe Saddam has been demonised and his Iraq with its malevolent security service maligned. Some political neophytes who have visited Iraq talk of the absence of any government monitors because they could not 'see' any. Most buy into the official Iraqi line that the United States is responsible for the suffering of the Iraqi people under sanctions and the destruction of this once-powerful, modern country, the most advanced and Westernised medically, scientifically and educationally in the region. The only answer is to remove sanctions, welcome Iraq back into the community of nations – which they believe is self-policing – and help rebuild the country. They have a telling argument in one respect. The neoleftists, joined in spirit for a short time by Republican conservative Richard Armey, charge that a war would be illegal under US and international law. They point out the implications at home and abroad if the US were to attack Iraq without sufficient provocation, without a UN mandate and without coalition backing. Furthermore, Armey points out, no war can occur without the advice and consent of Congress. They are, in my view, essentially correct, in particularly regarding the impact on American civil society and how Americans view their making of their foreign and defence policies. They are correct, too, in terms of the image of the United

States held by many people abroad living under the cloud of repressive regimes; for people who tend to believe in the principles of American governance without liking the American government, the US historically represented the rule of law, rights guaranteed in a written constitution, human rights, the right of citizens to enjoy and participate in a free and vibrant civil society.

The truth as defined by the K Street corridor: The mainstream think-tanks that line Washington's main streets – the Brookings Institution, the Carnegie Institute for Peace, the Center for Strategic and International Studies (CSIS), the Council on Foreign Relations, and even the Nixon Center for Peace and Freedom – are all venerable institutions representing the political centre, the slightly to the left of centre, or in the case of the Nixon Center, the moderate right. Wanting to have influence with whatever administration occupies the White House, they say that we can do Iraq but it will be costly in terms of money and manpower and, by the way, few of us have knowledge of Iraq, experience in the region, or a military background. Before deciding on war as the ultimate answer to our Iraq problem, they are exploring ways to make arms inspections more effective, what to do about people displaced by war, how to make smart sanctions smarter, and how to win over our European and Asian friends to our cause.

The truth as revealed by the regional special interest crowd: The Washington Institute for Near East Policy (WINEP) and the Middle East Institute (MEI) profess to be non-partisan in their research on appropriate policies for the US government to pursue regarding Iraq, but objectivity is in the eye of the beholder. Both are eloquent spokesmen for very special interests – WINEP speaks for Israel and its publications advocate policies as defined by Israeli officials and pro-Israeli researchers; MEI is no less an advocate for the Arab voice in US policy-making. WINEP has long been an advocate for the 'Iraq as Strategic Prize' thesis, the Iraqi National Congress (INC) and Chalabi, the creation and funding of an Iraqi Liberation Army, as well as regime change in Iran and Saudi Arabia. MEI until this spring worked with the State Department to bring together various elements that comprise the opposition to Saddam in exile, including the INC, the Iraqi National Accord and the many military and civilian Iraqi exiles with the skills, knowledge and desire to help rebuild Iraq after Saddam is gone.

Realities in US policy towards Iraq

All US governments have defined their policy choices regarding the Persian Gulf and Iraq in 'real' terms. It's the oil, even if we purchase less than 20% of our oil energy needs from Gulf states. It's the trade, even if we are not now a major trading partner of Iran or Iraq, and the total purchasing power of the six Gulf Cooperation Council (GCC) states cannot possibly purchase enough over time to sustain American economic growth. It's in our interest to preserve a balance of power in the region to protect our friends, even if they are autocrats who do not share our interests in democratic institutions, participatory democracy and human rights.

Similarly, US governments have had choices in how to deal with Iraq. In the 1980s, we provided military assistance when it seemed the revolutionary Islamic Republic of Iran would win the war and threaten not only Iraq but the fragile states of the GCC as well. The first Bush administration was loath to pursue charges of Iraq's use of chemical weapons or miserable human rights record because of the lure of trade and investment. Iraq's bullying of its Gulf Arab neighbours and invasion of Kuwait changed all that. Twelve years after the invasion of Kuwait and imposition of sanctions, American choices in dealing with Saddam and his regime – and conversely Iraqi options in dealing with the US – are narrowing as the rhetoric heats up and each side restates its non-negotiable position.

Saddam's position is that Iraq does not have a WMD capacity so all sanctions have to end now. His strategy of a diplomatic offensive resulted in the Arab summit's Beirut declaration in March 2002, which protested against an American attack on Iraq, called for an end to sanctions, and embraced Iraq as a reinstated member of the Arab fold. This diplomatic strategy is closely linked to an economic offensive that includes new deals with Russia and an expanding import-export construction, and cheap oil trade with Jordan, Syria, Turkey and Iran. All these governments have fragile economies dependent on doing business with Iraq. They understand Baghdad's warning that a war now would not only destroy Iraq's economy, it would place the fragile economies and governments of its neighbours at risk as well. The possibility that Saddam will do an about-face – as he did in 1975 when he decided to make peace with a stronger Iran to end the chronic Kurdish wars, at least temporarily, and concede to the Shah, also temporarily, his territorial demands in the Shatt al-Arab waterway – seems remote.

For Washington, the choices are few: impose sanctions on him, ignore him, accept him as the ultimate survivor, eliminate him, or pray someone else will. Sanctions and seeking to eliminate him as the ruler of Iraq are options the US is willing to pursue. Ignoring Saddam or accepting him, while preferable to some governments, remain unacceptable choices for the United States. Whatever the option, Saddam Hussein and the country he rules cannot be ignored, accepted, or eliminated without great risk.

Should sanctions-based policy continue? Sanctions initially were seen as a way to influence, shape, or modify the behaviour of a wayward state in much the same way as parents deal with a wayward child – you will not develop and use weapons of mass destruction, you will not frighten or invade your neighbour, you will not terrorise or oppress your people or any other people. Two kinds of sanctions were applied to Baghdad under terms of UNSCR 687 and 688 in April 1991: economic sanctions, which could be lifted when Iraq was found by the UN Security Council to be in compliance with the resolutions calling for elimination of its biological, chemical and nuclear weapons and long-range ballistic missiles; and a second set of sanctions that prohibits acquisition of military hardware and must be removed by a separate UN Security Council vote. Saddam Hussein must comply with UN Security Council Resolutions dictating Iraqi surrender for destruction all WMD programmes, stockpiles and sites, return to Kuwait all prisoners of war and stolen property and pay reparations to those harmed by his military occupation and near destruction of Kuwait. Saddam was also to end persecution of Iraq's so-called minorities – so-called because the 'minority' Shia Muslim Arabs comprise nearly 60% of the population of Iraq and the Kurds comprise approximately 20%.

Sanctions as policy were further refined by the administrations after George H.W. Bush. In 1993, the Clinton administration enshrined sanctions in its policy of dual containment. Dual containment was meant to force the 'rogue' states of Iran and Iraq to modify their behaviour and abide by international norms and UN Security Council resolutions.[6] Policy on Iraq became containment plus WMD inspections by UNSCOM, along with military operations when Iraq was found to be 'in breach' of the UNSCRs,[7] and at the end of the Clinton administration, regime change. Red lines for US military operations were also defined: if Saddam deployed weapons of mass destruction, if he threatened his neighbours and if he attacked the Kurds.

Sanctions worked in denying Saddam sovereignty and unfettered use of Iraq's oil revenues, in weakening his military and in denying him the ability to easily acquire components necessary to rebuild his weapons systems or reconstitute wholesale Weapons of Mass Destruction (WMD) programmes. Saddam has not been able to threaten his neighbours, although there have been military feints and rhetorical warnings against Kuwait and other governments allowing the United States access to military facilities. They have failed, however, in several critical respects. The result of sanctions and mostly desultory air strikes has been the impoverishment of Iraq's traditional middle class of bureaucrats, technocrats, intellectuals, professionals and civil servants; and higher mortality rates for the old, the weak, the children, and those otherwise undervalued or dispossessed by the regime (Shia areas of southern Iraq that had engaged in the 1991 rebellion, for example). Additional income received under the oil-for-food resolutions should have allowed Saddam to provide much-needed goods for Iraqis suffering under sanctions.[8] It did not. Nor have sanctions modified Saddam's behaviour. They have not changed his aggressive nature and the brutality of his regime, nor have they made him willing to forgo possession of his WMD. Their singular success was due to the consensus in the international community that sanctions were the proper tactic to apply until Saddam complied with UN resolutions.

Should sanctions-based policy end? Consensus on the utility of sanctions is eroding for several reasons. Firstly, the international ability to maintain inspections of imports and exports of goods to and from Iraq are almost certainly undermined by Baghdad's pliant neighbours, who prefer cheap oil, trade and contracts to import goods bound for Iraq. Secondly, Saddam has been able to divert international attention away from his internal policies of punishing potential opponents by withholding access to food and medicine and hoarding imported goods for his supporters. Instead, he blames the West – and specifically the US and the UK – for the deaths of Iraqi children, for the increased incidence of malnutrition and disease and for the impoverishment of the Iraqi middle class. Iraq's neighbours in the Arab world, members of the UN Security Council and many other governments have come to similar conclusions regarding the inefficacy of sanctions if not the culpability of the US.

Many regional and European governments, including former coalition partners France and Russia, agree that Iraq should allow UN weapons inspectors back into the country. They argue, however, against sanctions without end and without incentive. Nearly all the Arab and Muslim states oppose sanctions. The so-called Arab street and Islamist critics of Arab regimes sympathise with the Iraqi people, and Arab governments in increasing numbers are seeking ways to join the public consensus without openly forgiving Saddam. Dissent to sanctions policy and sympathy for Iraq's people is growing even in Riyadh and Kuwait City, bringing with it the risk of criticism of the regimes for maintaining the embargo at the expense of Arab and Muslim self-interest. Finally, Gulf Arab regimes once supportive of the progress made in Arab–Israeli relations since the Oslo and Madrid accords now feel very vulnerable with the collapse of the Palestinian–Israeli peace process and the visible violence of the *intifada*, which threatens to destroy Palestinian civil society. Perceived US unwillingness to rein in Israel threatens to unite the Arab world in opposition to US regional policies, including and especially regime change in Iraq and the war on terrorism.

If the endgame is to rid Iraq of its weapons of mass destruction, then Saddam's rule is not necessarily at issue. For Washington, however, Saddam is the issue. He is seen as the prime threat to regional security. US policymakers assume his objectives and behaviour are unlikely to change while he is in power. They say that only his removal will offer hope for change. They disagree with European and regional friends that are unwilling to support efforts at regime change and argue instead that policy change could occur under Saddam. They say they are willing to deal with him, although with considerable reserve. Why, American critics of European approaches to Saddam argue, should tactics that have failed before – engagement and incentives rather than containment and punishment – work now when they did not work earlier?

Can we ignore him? If you ignore or forgive Saddam, what then? Several questions must be answered by those who would ease or eliminate sanctions while Saddam remains in power and unrepentant. Without sanctions, what is at risk?

Iraq cannot be held accountable for compliance with UN Security Council resolutions, including those on monitoring its

WMD programmes. Without sanctions, Iraq has no reason to fear or abide by UN resolutions. Saddam effectively ended the UNSCOM monitoring and inspection regime by denying inspectors access to sites. He probably will do the same with UNMOVIC in Iraq now. Perceived disarray in the UN Security Council and higher oil revenues earned in the past two years give Saddam additional incentives to stonewall the UN as an institution while Baghdad courts energy-deprived Europe and Asia.[9]

Iraq will not comply with non-WMD requirements in the UN Security Council resolutions. The independent activities of UN humanitarian organisations and other international humanitarian relief organisations in monitoring equitable food and humanitarian aid distribution would not be permitted. Efforts to get Iraq to acknowledge and return Kuwaiti POWs or property or to pay reparations would be over. In early July, Saddam agreed to return to Kuwait its National Archives, a decision probably reflecting duress. The fate of nearly 700 missing Kuwaiti prisoners remains a mystery. Baghdad is likely to challenge the Kuwait–Iraq boundary settlement and the peacekeeping activities of the UN border commission, UNIKOM. Saddam warned Iraqis in a speech in August 2000 not to 'pay those to whom you are under no obligation more than their due'. This may have been a subtle hint at his unwillingness to continue to pay reparations, since it came at the same time as the Kuwait Petroleum Company presented its reparations claims. Payment into the compensation fund would become debt repayment to 'friends'. Money would be spent on domestic recovery, but few believe Saddam would delay military reconstruction for civilian redevelopment.

Saddam would not be a good neighbour in the region over the long term. To woo Arab friends and Muslim neighbours, Saddam in 2002 offered $25,000 to the families of Palestinian 'martyrs' and welcomed support from the Arab League. He sent emissaries to the GCC governments and welcomed their growing contacts and normalisation of diplomatic relations. In a speech one year ago, however, commemorating the end of the Iraq–Iran War, Saddam accused Turkey and the Gulf Arabs of 'treachery and disgrace' for harbouring the planes that kill the men, women and children of Iraq. He criticised 'those rulers and kings who have sold out their souls and appointed [the occupying foreigner] to rule over everything that is dear and precious in the values and wealth of their people'. Would he seek revenge? Saddam warned Iraqis *'not to provoke a snake before you make up your mind and muster up the ability to cut its head,'* and in vintage Saddam style, he warned Iraqis, *'Do not give your enemy any chance to get the upper hand of you… Do not exaggerate a promise you cannot fulfill or a threat your ability cannot support… Keep your eyes on your enemy. Be ahead of him but do not let him be far behind your back.'* In tones reminiscent of the prelude to the invasion in 1990, Baghdad occasionally claims Kuwait is once again digging wells and stealing oil from the oil fields that border the two countries. Saddam and his sons call for the armed overthrow of the Gulf regimes and any government providing support to the US military. And Saddam has reiterated his threats to attack Israel. The threats are similar to those issued in the spring of 1990 when Iraq warned Israel it would face 'incendiary weapons'.

Saddam would pursue weapons of mass destruction. He has done so while UNSCOM inspectors were operating in Iraq. It is possible to read Saddam's intentions in speeches made in the past two years. For example, on eliminating weapons systems, Saddam told officials of the Military Industrial Organisation in June 2000 that he was willing to limit weapons on condition that Israel did so first. The evidence lies in what Baghdad has been doing in the four years it has gone uninspected. Iraq has test-fired a short-range, liquid-fuelled ballistic missile – the *al-Samoud* ('resistance' in Arabic) – that could carry conventional explosives or the chemical or biological weapons that Iraq is still suspected of hiding.[10] US officials said the tests are evidence that Iraq is working to perfect its ballistic missile technology, which could be easily adapted to missiles with a longer range.

The ultimate reality: can or should Saddam and company be removed? Saddam's regime has survived crises that have destroyed governments facing similar problems. Wars, coup attempts, rebellions and loss of authority over 15 of 18 provinces in 1991, sanctions plus military operations and covert action plans thus far all have failed to remove Saddam and his regime. Diplomatic isolation has failed as more countries send airplanes and emissaries to, and trade with, Baghdad. Nor have the neighbours indicated any willingness to support military operations against Iraq. That was clearly the message delivered to Vice-President Cheney when he swept through the region in early 2002 and to President Bush by

Saudi Arabia's Crown Prince Abdullah and Jordan's King Abdullah. The GCC states might support a military operation if it were quick, surgical, decisive and under UN cover. Short of total success, however, they fear provoking Saddam anew by their opposition and are wary of domestic protests should they be seen to back American aggression against an Arab 'hero' and the suffering people of Iraq.

US efforts to re-invigorate Saddam's opponents in exile have met with mixed results. Recriminations over past 'betrayals' – from the Kurdish parties, the Shia who rebelled in 1991 and the INC – have masked the inability of the groups in active, organised opposition to Baghdad to work together. The US government has dealt with the INC since its inception as an umbrella opposition group in 1993. While many of the estimated 3 million Iraqis living in exile support efforts to remove him, they refuse to coalesce under the banner of the INC. Leadership rivalries and disagreements over tactics – should we accept US money, should we plan a military response to fight Saddam, should we meet on Iraqi soil – keep the camps at odds. There is not one Iraqi opposition – there are several oppositions based in London, Damascus, Paris, Amman, Washington and elsewhere. Where they are not is Iraq. It is impossible to evaluate their claims to have connections to or supporters in Iraq. Indeed, with the exception of a few representatives of well-known traditional families, few are known or respected in Iraq.

The key elements missing to make a credible opposition with the INC are the Kurds and the Shia. The two major Kurdish factions – the Kurdish Democratic Party led by Massoud Barzani and the Patriotic Union of Kurdistan led by Jalal Talabani – remain outside the INC although they both have representatives on the executive board. The major Shia opposition group – the Supreme Council for the Islamic Revolution in Iraq (SCIRI) – is led by an Iraqi Arab cleric, Ayatollah Muhammad Baqr al-Hakim, and based in Iran. SCIRI is not part of the INC, although a representative in London attends some meetings. The Kurds and the Shia are the war-fighters of the Iraqi opposition; without them operating against the regime in Iraq, there is no Iraqi Liberation Army. They have apparently come together in a grouping dubbed the 'Gang of Four'. It is not yet clear if they intend this to replace the INC, cooperate with the INC or actually undertake anti-regime operations. A key shift in SCIRI policy may have been signalled in August 2002 when Abd al-Aziz al-Hakim, a leader of the organisation's paramilitary wing and the brother of its leader Muhammad Baqr al-Hakim, joined the representatives of five other opposition groups for talks in Washington.

Risks and opportunities for US policy: the scenarios

Risks and opportunities abound in the options the Bush administration is considering if and when it goes to war with Iraq. Clear proponents of one plan refuse to acknowledge the risks inherent in their plan or the opportunities presented by another one. The American people are clearly becoming equally confounded. While most Americans want to support their president and fully back the war on terrorism, doubt about the wisdom or necessity of war with Iraq is clearly growing. A *CNN–USA Today* poll, with results published in November 2001, and March, June and August 2002, found that in June 83% of Americans polled believed removing Saddam should be a top US foreign policy goal (down from 88% in March 2002); 59% said the US should take military action in Iraq (down from 74% in November 2001); while 34% were against invasion. More recent figures in August show the trend continuing: 53% favoured a US military operation against Iraq, while the percentage of those polled who opposed an attack had risen to 45%.[11]

The problem with the Afghan model. Iraq is not Afghanistan. It is not a failed state nor one bereft of population centres used to protect high-valued regime targets. Air power and smart bombs will be insufficient to achieve the mission without the additional use of a significant number of ground forces. The fighting will be in cities and towns, and not desert caves. Significant civilian casualties (called collateral damage), property damage and the destruction once again of Iraq's power grids, economic infrastructure and daily life is certain. An international conference in Bonn, in which Iran played a key role in bringing the parties to the table before the Afghan campaign, helped to identify a potential interim leader – Hamid Karzai – and set the terms for an interim government. Where is the Karzai for Iraq? Where is Iran? And where is the opposition inside the country with experience in fighting a weak and central authority? Iraq's Kurdish and Shia paramilitary groups based in northern Iraq and Iran are not the equivalent of the Northern Alliance; the Kurds have spend most of their military energy fighting each other and Shia dissidents have managed only small, isolated operations against Iraqi units. General Anthony Zinni, Franks' predecessor as Commander-in-Chief of CENTCOM, refused to consider arming, training and bringing the Iraqi opposition along to fight Baghdad. His oft-quoted remark that to do so would create a 'Bay of Goats' distracted attention away from his other singular point, that for a successful campaign there would have to be an American-led and -fought campaign. Protecting an inexperienced, untested force of former silk suits, he noted, would only place American forces at risk.

Conflicting goals among our Kurdish 'allies': We have pledged significant military support to protect the safety of the three predominantly-Kurdish northern provinces, which have made remarkable progress at economic reconstruction, if not reconstitution of political authority. In the event of an attack by US forces, would the Kurds fight against Baghdad? Or would they stay north of the 36th parallel, except to try and seize Kirkuk? Will they heed our support for the territorial integrity and political unity of Iraq? The Kurds say they want a federal solution – does that mean regional autonomy or self-rule for the Kurds but not for the Turkoman, Assyrian or other minorities having similar and conflicting claims to territory and self-rule in northern Iraq?

Can we bring real democracy or only democratic-sounding institutions to Iraq and will the Iraqis welcome this? What do the Iraqis inside the country want? Iraqis probably will welcome the US once they are sure Saddam and sons are gone. What they may not welcome is an imposed solution with a government hand-picked by Washington, and they will not welcome a foreign military presence that overstays its welcome. Iraqis in the military and the civil government and members of prominent tribes, clans and factions, all of whom have long been encouraged to overthrow Saddam's regime, may choose to stay home and wait out the war. They will want assurance that the old regime is really dead and that the US will stay to help establish a new government. Most Iraqis probably will not welcome 'outsiders' – meaning the Iraqis of the diaspora – taking over power and authority, and most probably will not be reassured if we turn the reins of government over to prominent tribal, military or party leaders who abandon the regime in the last minute to join US efforts and then demand reward for their sacrifice and risk. The opportunity to create a pluralistic political system, representative government and democratic institutions is a powerful incentive that could be placed in jeopardy by turning government over too quickly to the 'wrong' Iraqis.

What will the neighbours think? The neighbourhood plan has been somewhat more muted and less democratic than the US plan. Most of Iraq's neighbours – including possibly Iran – seem to prefer an ABS system: Anyone But Saddam. If we are going to have regime change, let it be a regime we can live with. Political change need not be deep or wide. We agree with the US that no son, no family member, no Tikritis, no Ba'athists need apply, but we are also uneasy with your concept of democratic rule, coalition politics and political pluralism – after all, we are not democrats and see no need for these things at home, so why in Iraq? Coalition government has never survived the heat in Iraq, we mistrust Kurdish ambitions for self-rule leading to independence from Baghdad, and pluralism with one person, one vote will only mean the Shia dominance of Iraq's political institutions. These are unacceptable risks. For the sake of stability, 'we' (and this includes Iran in the short-term) prefer a Sunni Arab general in concert with a coalition of military and civilian leaders of prominence – no pluralism, no warlordism, no chaos and no spill-over. Iran in the longer term would prefer a pluralistic solution that brings the Shia to majority status, and it may try to force the return of the nearly one million Iraqi refugees it has sheltered since Saddam's forced expulsions in the 1980s and the Gulf wars. Political stability in Iran at this juncture is somewhat uncertain, although all Iranians regardless of political persuasion, are liable to feel threatened by the presence of a pro-US government in Baghdad.

What should the US do?

If the United States is determined to use military operations to effect regime change in Iraq, then the administration needs to review its options. What is the mission – just eliminating Saddam and his cohort or establishing a democratic coalition and representative government in Iraq? What size force will be needed and how long will it have to be positioned in Iraq after Saddam is removed? What Iraqi 'opposition' do we deal with – the INC, which lacks credibility with most Iraqis, a son or general of Saddam's on the theory that Anyone But Saddam is fine as long as it is someone who can impose law and order on the capital and the country? And, perhaps most importantly, what is the risk to regional stability if and when Saddam is removed? What will be the impact if one Sunni Arab replaces another Sunni Arab in Baghdad? Or if a democratic coalition leading to elections and theoretically a Shia majority in government results? Or, the most frightening and perhaps most likely of scenarios – what if warlordism arises in Iraq, with factions and tribes, ethnic and sectarian violence creating chaos and disorder?

What should the US response be to these scenarios? It is clear that to ignore Saddam and Iraq's flaunting of the UN and international law is to encourage him. If the governments supporting US operations – the UK, Kuwait, Turkey and occasionally Saudi Arabia – withdraw their support, as they threaten to do, then do we go it alone? Can we complete the mission without a regional ally? We may be able to do so, but we will need the clear and open support of the neighbours and the members of our old anti-Saddam coalition to ensure that Iraq after Saddam remains intact and moves towards stable, democratic political institutions, economic reform and a restrained military with no WMD ambitions.

Should the US be prepared to recognise a son or a general of Saddam should he die or be removed from power? This is an important issue. Does US policy change if only Saddam is gone? US policy choices could be determined by the way in which Saddam 'goes'. If he dies because of illness – rumors that he has cancer or is senile circulate regularly – or old age, then he will have had time to arrange a succession of his choice. Perhaps Saddam has learned some lessons in the transfer of power in Iraq by observing the process in Syria. Bashar al-Assad was a relative political unknown with a reputation for opposing corruption and favouring technocrats and modernisation. Sadam's eldest son Uday cannot be transformed from a figure of fear and loathing into one of sympathy, education and strength. His second son Qusay, who has been the less visible but equally lethal of the sons, has lately surfaced not just as head of Saddam's multiple security forces, but has begun speaking out publicly on political matters.[12] If there is time to plan the transition, then Qusay will be able to place loyalists in positions of power and authority and eliminate any immediate challengers, including his brother. This might ensure a relatively stable succession process. It will not, however, satisfy Washington.

If Qusay is the successor, then the US will have to decide whether it can deal with a son of the regime it has declared rogue. Qusay appears to be very much like his father – a cunning and suspicious figure who trusts no one and places survival of the regime above Iraq's security and well-being. He may be willing to offer vague concepts of reform, broaden the base of government and accept some limits on Iraqi actions, but he will not compromise on Iraq's independence, territorial sovereignty or right to defend Iraq's national interest, however he may define it.

A coup by military or political factions that removed Saddam might be more tolerable for US policymakers. It would certainly be welcomed by Iraq's neighbours and by European and Asian governments longing to deal with Baghdad again. Their rush to approve could pre-empt the impact of a US decision to recognise, not recognise or delay recognition to influence Baghdad's new government. If Saddam is overthrown by a revolt, then it is likely that blood revenge against and among the family – as well as rival cousins and clans – would eliminate Uday, Qusay and others from the more disreputable side of the family. Iraq's neighbours would hope that by quick recognition of the successor government they would shore up a sufficiently strong successor who could hold the country together. They would have little interest in the form of government to be reconstructed in Iraq, so long as it were led by a Sunni Arab military figure with little interest in sharing power with the Shias or extending autonomy to the Kurds.

Going It Alone. Pursuit of a foreign policy dominated by an Iraq agenda could have serious consequences for other US policies and interests. What is the price Washington is willing to pay to ensure international – or P-5 (Permanent five members of the UN Security Council) – solidarity or quiescence if America attacks Iraq? Do we compromise on the war on terrorism? Do we offer Russia concessions on missile defence, guarantees that the oil contracts signed with Saddam's regime will be honoured by his successor, or loans? We could ease up on other sanctioned states, such as Iran and Cuba, in return for European support for our Iraq policy. In the short term, we probably will continue to have support from the UK and France on upholding the UN Security Council resolutions. But Paris and Moscow will also push for easing restrictions, allowing trade and opening the country to development and investment. I once assumed that none would support military operations in Iraq, but that was before the events of 11 September and the eagerness of many governments to join the war on terrorism, albeit for their own self-interest. It is rumoured that Russia, Turkey and France will support a military operation on Iraq; it seems the UK is with us but pressure on Blair to reconsider his blanket support for US policy initiatives is growing.

The United States may in the longer term have to 'go it alone'. Without a war and without the support of other governments, it will be impossible to maintain a hard-line policy on Iraq, including sanctions, after Saddam is gone. The US needs to have policies now for the time when change comes to Iraq, for it will probably come unannounced and undeterred by outside events. The US will have to decide whether it can deal with any successor and whether it is prepared to waive UN Security Council resolutions and end economic sanctions in return for a promise of stability, lessened tensions with neighbours, and an end to the persecution of Iraq's people. The US will need to remind the Kurds of their commitment to remain within Iraq and that we are not prepared to support a Kurdish entity independent of Baghdad. It will need to remind the neighbours – Iran, Syria, Turkey and Saudi Arabia – of their commitments to respect the integrity of Iraq and warn them not to interfere as Iraq's ethnic, sectarian, tribal and institutional factions determine the make-up of a post-Saddam Iraq. And it must be prepared to stay the course, once the regime is changed.

Regardless of who or what replaces Saddam and company, the US will have to follow a consistent and coherent policy towards Iraq. Declaring red lines, threatening war to support regime change and then ignoring Baghdad's egregious behaviour will encourage a successor of Saddam to act more aggressively towards his neighbours and Iraqis in pursuit of his goals. Several policy guidelines seem appropriate:

- Do not threaten military action unless you are serious in applying a military solution. And do not promise military attack until and unless you have considered the options and consequences for US and regional interests.
- Don't declare objective goals that are impossible to accomplish (such as claiming military operations are intended

to eliminate all WMD stocks, programmes and facilities). Don't arm an opposition that is not a credible threat or support an opposition just to annoy Saddam; they aren't and it won't.

- Decide what kind of successor you are willing to accept and be prepared to follow through as events unfold. This assumes that policymakers must decide how important it is to US interests and regional stability to keep Iraq stable rather than see it slip into chaos or civil war.

- Consider rapprochement with Iran before an attack on Iraq and while calibrating the kind of government a post-Saddam Iraq will have.

- Finally, the US must be prepared to maintain its commitments to regional security, to Iraqi stability and to the GCC states.

As a final note, let me simply list the unknowable:

- The Bush administration has not made clear its justification and evidence for an attack, but it will not be just about oil or WMD or even terrorism. For some the issue is simply to bring democracy to Iraq and hence to remake the region in Iraq's image.

- What is the capability and what is the vision of the Iraqi military today – the Regular Army, Republican Guard, Ba'ath Party militias? What will it be after Saddam? And, since we are determined to deny any Iraqi regime WMD, will you allow the new Baghdad to rebuild its conventional military? It seems to me that, if you insist on the former, you must allow the latter.

- What would Iraqis do if/when we attack – what would convince them that they no longer have Saddam to fear, or put another way, that hope for liberation outweighs living under Saddam? At what point will Iraqis act? Or, are they no longer capable of acting to preserve their country, values and hopes for the future?

- What progress has Iraq made in advancing its WMD acquisition, research and development since inspections ended in the summer of 1998?

- Is there in Iraq a Sunni Arab general with Shia cousins, a Turkoman brother-in-law, and a Kurdish grandmother who was a war hero (doesn't matter which war) and who will relinquish control to civilian authority and an elected government with participatory democracy, democratic institutions, and human rights?

Notes

Judith S. Yaphe is a senior research fellow in the Institute for National Strategic Studies at the National Defense University, Washington, DC. The comments and conclusions of this paper are hers and do not reflect those of the university, the Department of Defense or any other government agency.

1 The neocons have received considerable press coverage as the war of words on Iraq and other Middle East policy issues has heated up in Washington. See for example Joshua Micah Marshall, 'The Pentagon's Internal War', *Salon,* 9 August 2002.

2 UNSCOM was the United Nations Special Commission, which detected, inspected and destroyed much of Iraq's chemical and nuclear weapons programme from the end of the Gulf War in 1991 until 1997, when Saddam stopped allowing inspections. UNMOVIC, the United Nations Monitoring, Verification and Inspection Commission is the new version of UNSCOM created by the Security Council in 1998 to replace UNSCOM, which is supposed to operate with the same authority to conduct unannounced full and unfettered inspections.

3 See, for example, his speech on 26 August 2002 to a Veterans of Foreign Wars convention, 'Cheney Says Peril of a Nuclear Iraq Justifies Attack', *The New York Times,* 27 August 2002, p. A1.

4 In an editorial in *The Washington Post* in late June 2002, James Hoagland called on the Bush administration to 'be muscular'. In breathless prose, Hoagland claimed that: 'The US presence will serve as the linchpin for democratic transformation of a major Arab country that can be a model for the region' as well as a source of energy security for Americans. 'No Time to Think Small', *The Washington Post,* June 30, 2002, p. B7.

5 See David Ochmanek's paper in this volume.

6 Sanctions against Iran sought to persuade it to abandon support for international terrorism, end its opposition to the Arab–Israeli peace process and end its quest for weapons of mass destruction.

7 Military operations could be authorised when Iraq was found to be 'in breach' of UN Security Council resolutions — the term is included in UNSCR 687 and was to be applied when Saddam banned or otherwise obstructed UNSCOM in its inspection activities.

8 Saddam accepted the first oil-for-food resolution, UNSCR 986, which allowed Iraq to sell $1.8 billion in oil every six months in 1996, five years after it was first proposed. He almost certainly did so because he was unable to supply his loyal support base in the military and security services. By 1999, the amount of oil Iraq could sell had risen to $5.2bn every six months and then to virtually whatever it could sell.

9 US government officials estimated that Iraq earned $18bn in oil revenue last year because of high prices and the tight market. This is more than Iraq was earning in 1990, on the eve of the Kuwait invasion. Although the revenues go to the escrow

account at the UN, the additional money gives Saddam more bargaining room with contractors and energy consumers.

[10] The range of the missile was less than 150 kilometres (95 miles), thus not in violation of UN Security Council resolutions that ban missiles with a range greater than 150km.

[11] Andrea Stone, 'Poll: 59% say US should take military action in Iraq', *USA Today*, 21 June 2002, p. 8A. 519 people were polled with a margin of error of +/- 5 percentage points. See polls of 21 June 2002 and 22 August 2002.

[12] In a letter to his father sent on the occasion of the 10th anniversary of the occupation of Kuwait, Qusay applauded the 'decisive role' of the Republican Guard, which he heads, in the 'liberation' of Kuwait. Iraqi opposition sources may be over-interpreting Qusay's motives, but he could be making a bid for a more open political role to rival his brother's election to the parliament in April 2000 by 99% of the vote.

Chapter 2

A Possible US-Led Campaign Against Iraq: Key Factors and an Assessment

David Ochmanek

This paper provides an overview of a postulated US-led military campaign against Iraq that could be undertaken in the early months of 2003. Its purpose is to specify the key determinants of such a campaign and to offer some judgements about how an operation against Iraq might unfold, as a basis for discussion of the possible consequences of the conflict and its aftermath. The views offered here are not informed by access to any official planning efforts or direct contact with policymakers or military officers involved in the development of US military options *vis à vis* Iraq.

Objectives

President Bush and senior members of his administration have been quite clear in outlining US objectives regarding Iraq. They seek 'regime change', motivated primarily by Saddam Hussein's persistent refusal to comply with UN-mandated prohibitions on the development and possession of chemical, biological and nuclear weapons. The administration is animated not just by the prospect of a re-militarised Iraq armed with these weapons (and appropriate delivery systems), but perhaps more so by the possibility that Saddam or his successors might permit a terrorist organisation, such as al-Qaeda, to gain access to these weapons. The goal of a war on

Iraq, then, would be to eliminate the possibility that Iraq could become a source of chemical, biological, radiological or nuclear (CBRN) weapons. This would mean, in the short term, taking down Saddam's regime, rounding up its principals, occupying the entire country and rooting out the infrastructure devoted to the development of the proscribed weapons. In the longer term, the United States and others in the international community would have to assist the people of Iraq in overhauling their political system and establishing a reformed political and strategic culture conducive to stability within Iraq and the surrounding region.

For Saddam Hussein's part, we must assume that, confronted with the threat of invasion and occupation, his overriding objective would be survival. Here, the goals of personal survival, the survival of the regime and the defeat of the invasion are inextricably connected: If foreign forces succeed in occupying Iraq, it is difficult to imagine Saddam and his coterie escaping capture for long. One assumes that Saddam's secondary objectives, if the invasion could somehow be thwarted, would remain what they have been in the past – to remain in charge of an Iraq that retains the sinews of national power and wields commensurate influence in the region and beyond. This, in turn, means consolidating the regime's control over Iraq's territory and society, modernising the armed forces and resuming work on CBRN weapons.

Requisites for success

A US-led military operation against Iraq would be shaped by a number of political realities that, collectively, would constitute important determinants of a successful campaign. Chief among these are:

- **Rapid achievement of military and political objectives**. Even if Washington succeeds in winning some form of UN mandate for the operation, opposition to a military campaign will be intense and widespread, particularly in the Muslim world. This places a premium on a campaign characterised by early and rapid movement of forces into Iraq to liberate large areas.

- **Minimal civilian casualties**. The same considerations, plus the ubiquity of the international media, mean that the attacking forces must do everything possible to minimise the suffering that their operations impose upon Iraqi civilians. Likewise, intensive efforts will be called for to ensure that Saddam cannot successfully lash out at civilian populations in surrounding countries – principally, Kuwait, Turkey, and any other states that might permit US and allied forces to operate from their territories, and, of course, Israel.

- **Minimal friendly casualties**. The premise for this operation is that it is better to face the costs and risks of an attack now than to wait while Saddam builds ever more dangerous capabilities. The wisdom of that course of action may be called into question if the casualties associated with the operation are very high (say, fatalities in the thousands).

- **Minimal casualties to regular Iraqi army units**. US and allied leaders acknowledge the important differences between Iraq's largely conscripted regular army and the units staffed by hand-picked loyalists, especially the Special Republican Guard (SRG), but also the Republican Guard (RG). To avoid punishing ordinary soldiers and to sustain a core of trained manpower that might help stabilise the country in the post-conflict period of reconstruction, US and allied forces would seek to secure the surrender of most Iraqi military units with a minimum of bloodshed.

- **Minimal damage to civil infrastructure**. The operations being considered against Iraq are not coercive campaigns designed to alter the leadership's decision-making calculus. Rather, they are intended to strip away the regime's defences in order to eliminate it. As such, attacks on infrastructure targets would be useful only insofar as they would impede the conduct of defensive operations within Iraq or promote feelings that the defeat of the regime was inevitable. In general, then, attacks on infrastructure would be avoided, both to strengthen the moral case for the war and to facilitate postwar recovery efforts.

If Saddam is to have a chance of defeating the attack, he must try to prevent allied forces from achieving the operational outcomes outlined above. Most importantly, he must forestall the collapse of his defences while seeking to mobilise international pressure on the attackers. He will want, above all, to preserve a potent ground force 'in being' that attacking forces must contend with in order to gain control of the Iraqi heartland running from Tikrit through Baghdad and into the other heavily populated areas of the Tigris-Euphrates plain. In addition, Saddam would seek to impose casualties on attacking forces, both within Iraq and in operational rear areas. And he would strive to prevent his enemies from conducting a 'clean' campaign that avoids civilian casualties and damage to civil infrastructures. Towards this end, one must expect that Iraqi military forces and assets would be deployed in close proximity to civilians when possible. Likewise, incidents of collateral damage would be amplified through propaganda.

Iraqi forces (See the appendix for a listing of Iraqi military forces.) Iraq's forces today are, of course, considerably weaker overall than those that the coalition faced in 1990–91. At the same time, however, it must be remembered that Iraq's forces in a prospective conflict would be called upon to do different things in a different (and potentially more favourable) operating environment than that of the Gulf War. Most importantly, Iraqi forces in the war being considered here would not be seeking to seize or hold terrain. Knowing that they cannot prevail against allied mechanised forces in a campaign of manoeuver and that they are at grave risk from air attack if they concentrate in the open, they would presumably avoid such operations.

Iraq's ground forces can be conceived of as being arrayed roughly in concentric circles around Baghdad. The most politically reliable forces – the Special Republican Guard (SRG) – are said to be deployed within Baghdad and have as their primary mission protection of the regime. The next most reliable and capable units – those of the Republican Guard (RG) – are generally found on the outskirts of Baghdad and well away from the northern and southern no-fly zones being imposed by US and British air forces. Units of the regular army are normally deployed along the periphery of the country. In the north the bulk of these forces are reportedly arrayed along the borders with the Kurdish zones in northeastern Iraq; in the southeast they are engaged in operations against the Shia and along the Kuwaiti border.[1]

Postulated campaign strategy

According to press reports, US thinking about a campaign against Iraq has evolved considerably over the past nine months or so. In the immediate aftermath of the surprisingly swift victory over the Taliban in Afghanistan, civilian officials in the US Department of Defense (DoD) were said to have been intrigued with the possibility of taking down Saddam Hussein's regime with a similar operation, dubbed by some the 'Afghan option'. This approach would rely heavily on indigenous forces within Iraq, leavened by US and allied special forces and heavily supported by precision air attacks, to take on units loyal to the regime. In this concept, masses of friendly troops would compel forces loyal to Saddam to concentrate in defence of specific objectives, making these forces vulnerable to attack from the air. Attack aircraft would be guided to their targets by orbiting airborne sensors and by US and allied forward controllers attached to anti-Saddam Iraqi units.

The difficulty of this approach, of course, is that it is far from clear where the required masses of friendly indigenous forces would come from. Apart from some fissiparous Kurdish groups in the north and some lightly armed Shia scattered in the south, the United States and its allies would have to depend on the large-scale defection of units from the Iraqi army to rally to the cause – a fairly dubious proposition. And even if such defections occurred, it is not clear that these newfound allies would have the commitment or the capacity to prosecute effective operations against any hard core of forces loyal to Saddam. The inability or unwillingness of Afghan forces to root hundreds of al-Qaeda fighters out of their redoubts in Tora Bora or to interdict their retreat offered a cautionary example of the drawbacks of over-reliance on local forces to take on hard fighting.

Partly out of a sense of alarm over the Afghan option, planners at the United States' Central Command (CENTCOM) headquarters are said to have presented a much more conventional approach for overthrowing Saddam. This plan, characterised as a 'minimum risk' approach, called for an invasion by approximately seven divisions, supported by fixed- and rotary-wing air assets. The aim was to overwhelm Iraqi ground forces swiftly and drive on Baghdad along three axes of advance from the north, south and west. The civilian leadership at DoD was said to have regarded this plan as ponderous and unattractive. The judgment was that too many of the United States' ground force units and logistics support assets would have to be brought from other regions and other operations to execute an operation of this magnitude, and too much time would be required to deploy the forces into position. The plan also envisaged the deployment of large numbers of US ground forces in countries surrounding Iraq – something that seemed increasingly unlikely as Arab dissatisfaction has grown over Washington's policies regarding the second Palestinian *intifada*. Moreover, the plan was said to have downplayed, if not ignored, the role that advanced air forces and reconnaissance assets could play in locating and neutralising Iraqi forces.

What will almost certainly emerge from these efforts is a hybrid plan that falls somewhere between the 'Afghan' option and the 'minimum risk' option in terms of the number and types of forces called for and the risks associated with the operation. Such an intermediate option might feature some or all of the following phases:

1. **Large-scale air attacks**. The operation would very likely commence with several days of large-scale, but precisely focused air attacks. Initial targets would consist of command-and-control sites associated with Iraq's integrated air defence system (IADS), as well as airfields and any SAM systems that could be located. Simultaneously, strikes would be unleashed on sites thought to be used for the storage or manufacture of CBRN weapons and longer-range ballistic missiles. National-level leadership facilities and their associated communications would also be struck in an effort to disrupt Saddam's ability to exert control over the nation and his forces. Garrisons and barracks associated with the RG and SRG would also be attacked as sorties were available, as would elements of national infrastructure that might be used to support defensive military operations (e.g., selected petroleum, oil, and lubricants storage and distribution facilities, some electrical power generation and key bridges along strategic lines of communication).

2. **Combined arms offensive**. Mechanised ground forces would jump off from points in Kuwait and Turkey towards objectives in the southeastern and northern parts of Iraq. The immediate goals of these operations would be to seize control of large areas of the

country, including Basra and Kirkuk, and to encircle regular army units in the hope of gaining their surrender with minimal fighting. If these objectives could be achieved quickly, efforts would be made to establish the beginnings of an interim political administration in captured territories. From these centers, forces would begin to press outward, enlarging zones of liberation.

3. Psychological and information operations. Intensive efforts would be made to rally military and security forces, elites and populations, both within captured areas and beyond, in opposition to the regime. The allies would seek to depict the defeat of Iraq's armed forces as inevitable. They would provide assurances regarding post-war political arrangements. And they would communicate their intention to hold persons who employ CBRN weapons or who violate the laws of war personally responsible for those actions. US forces would also seek to sow confusion in the ranks of the Iraqi high command by inserting disinformation into the Iraqi picture of the unfolding strategic, operational and tactical situation.

4. 'Creative improvisation'. US planners would hope at this point that organised resistance to the invasion would begin to crumble. This is the scenario that General Barry McCaffrey, who commanded the US 24th Infantry Division in the Gulf War, has in mind when he states his belief that a future invasion of Iraq can succeed within 21 days as Iraqi forces begin to 'unravel' under the pressure of the offensive.[2] However, for this to occur, units close to Saddam would have to begin to lose cohesion and confidence even though they may not have suffered significant damage. For if units of the SRG, RG and other elements of the security apparatus are dispersed prior to the commencement of the air attacks and if they remain deployed largely in urbanised areas, US and allied military forces would find it difficult to bring large-scale firepower to bear against them.

Because the reactions of such forces cannot be predicted in advance, US and allied forces will have to be prepared to combat more or less intact units of infantry and special forces, many of which could be deployed in urban areas. Doubtless, the allies would continue to try to press selective air attacks on forces and command centres that can be located, either by remote means or by spotters on the ground, if such attacks can be prosecuted with modest risks to civilians. Allied forces would also have the option of, in essence, laying siege to large areas in the hope of cutting off the enemy forces within from needed supplies. Such an approach would be viable, however, only if the civilians within these areas were able to escape and if the military forces remaining within collapsed fairly quickly. Both tactics could be supplemented with small-scale raids by heliborne assault forces on high value targets, such as military headquarters. And it might be possible for armoured and mechanised ground forces to 'slice off' one or more large sections of the urban hedgehog, cutting off the forces within from central command and control and resupply. All of these approaches and more would likely be tried before allied forces would be directed to take on the demanding and risky task of reducing enemy forces (possibly equipped with chemical and biological weapons) in urban terrain.

5. Occupation and administration. Defeating Iraqi military forces, of course, is but a means to the larger ends of regime change and dismantling the infrastructure of CBRN weapons. Saddam and his entourage will have to be hunted down and killed or captured. As Manuel Noriega showed us in Panama, this can prove difficult and time consuming even after organised military resistance has collapsed. In the meantime, the massive effort of providing for the needs of millions of displaced Iraqis and, then, creating a secure environment for post-war reconstruction would begin.

Assessment

A first order estimate of the forces that might be called for to conduct an operation of this magnitude is provided in the appendix. In brief, it is a smaller but considerably 'smarter' version of the forces that conducted Operation Desert Storm in 1991. These forces should have little trouble achieving the objectives of the opening phases of the operation, provided adequate basing is available.[3] Iraq's air defences would probably be able to prevent allied air forces from having free reign over the core of the country for several weeks, but they would not be able to impose levels of attrition on attacking aircraft that would be prohibitive. Improved reconnaissance and rapid targeting capabilities would enable allied air forces to locate and strike high value targets with greater effectiveness than in 1991, but even so, air attacks alone will not be able to eliminate leadership, WMD, *Scud* missiles and other critical targets comprehensively.

Phase 4 – the reduction of the SRG and other forces in the core of the country – is *terra incognita* and it is here that the outcome of the operation would be judged as either a bargain or, perhaps, a very costly 'success.' Assessing the outcome of this phase has at least as much to do with psychology as with military science. It would turn on several key issues:

- **The loyalty, training, and cohesion of the SRG, RG and other special forces**. It is difficult to maintain control over units that are dispersed in urban environments. Iraqi commanders would therefore find it challenging to keep tabs on forces under them and to compel them to fight once they began to engage US forces. If US and allied forces were able to create a sense of inevitability about the outcome of the conflict, even highly disciplined units remaining in the cities might begin to melt away. Alternatively, the possibility that many individuals and small units would fight tenaciously cannot be ruled out.

- **The willingness and ability of Iraqi forces to employ chemical and biological weapons effectively and on a large scale**. Actually employing CW and BW poses a host of risks (personal and operational) for the attacker and, needless to say, for any civilians that might be in the conflict zone. If Saddam were to order their use (and it must be assumed that he would), it is not clear that his orders would be widely followed. However, even the possibility of encountering chemical or biological agents would compel US and allied forces to adopt defensive and protective measures that would reduce the effectiveness and endurance of individual soldiers in and near areas of combat.

- **The attitude and actions of the Iraqi populace – especially the Sunnis – both in liberated areas and in those areas still controlled by loyal troops**. If things break in the allies' favour, General McCaffrey's prediction of a three-week operation with only modest levels of fighting and casualties could prove accurate. If not, one could conceive of a conflict that took months to resolve and which led to tens of thousands of casualties on both sides as well as serious suffering on the part of Iraqi civilians in the areas of the core fighting. Once committed to an operation with stakes of this magnitude, the United States and its allies would surely do whatever was necessary to prevail, even (or especially) if the worst happened and their forces got bogged down in a lengthy fight in which CW and/or BW were unleashed. The question, then, is less one of whether Saddam would be unseated by such an operation than one of the human and policy costs that the conflict would exact.

Finally, if something like the conflict outlined here does occur and the United States and its allies succeed in defeating the Iraqi armed forces, deposing Saddam and his regime, and occupying all of Iraq, success in the true endgame – providing a secure environment for the remaking of the political system and culture of Iraq – cannot simply be assumed. The emergence of tribally-based or ethnically-based insurgent or terrorist groups unreconciled to the post-Saddam order cannot be ruled out, particularly if the regime in Iran chose to sponsor and harbour such groups. In any case, the state of social science (if it can be called that) is such that we have only the most general notions of how to proceed in a project of this magnitude. It is very difficult to estimate the level of resources called for, other than to recognise that the demands will be high and that the work would go on for perhaps a generation or longer. Whether this administration or the international community are up to the challenge is unclear, though recent experience with the 'stability phase' and post-war reconstruction in Afghanistan is thus far not encouraging.

Appendix

Iraqi Forces, 2002

Ground forces
16 regular army divisions (6 heavy), all at 50% combat effectiveness or less
Plus: 5 commando brigades and 2 special forces brigades
6 Republican Guard (RG) divisions (3–5 heavy)
4 Special Republican Guard (SRG) brigades
Total armor: Approx. 5,200 vehicles, less than one-half operable
Very limited mobile logistics assets
62 armed helicopters

These military units are supplemented by extensive internal security forces, paramilitary units, border guards, and special police, all of which share responsibilities for regime protection. Total paramilitary manpower = 42–44,000.

Air forces
316 combat aircraft (incl. MiG-23BN, Mirage F1EQ5, Su-20, Su-22 M, Su-24 MK, Su-25, F-&, MiG 21, MiG-23, MiG-25, Mirage F-1EQ, MiG-29). Operational readiness rates are thought to be between 50% and 60%.

Air defences
SAM some 850 launches SA-2/ -3/ -6/ -7/ -8/ -9/ -13/ 14/ -16, *Roland, Aspide*
AD Guns   3,000

Missile forces
As many as 6 Scud launchers with perhaps   12 *al-Hussein* (650km) and a small force of *al-Samoud* missiles (200km).
Chemical and biological weapons.

Source: The Military Balance 2002•2003, IISS

Postulated US and UK forces for an offensive campaign against Iraq

Ground forces
2 corps comprised of 5+ divisions (Army and Marine Corps) (3+ heavy, 1+ air assault, 1 light infantry, 7 - 8 SOF battalions, including civil affairs units).
Extensive logistics augmentation.

Air forces
5–6 wings of land-based combat aircraft (approx. 400 total)
3 carrier air wings (approx. 150 total combat aircraft)
Approx. 40 heavy bombers
200+ air refueling aircraft
Numerous airborne surveillance and intra-theater airlift aircraft

Missile defences
6–8 Patriot battalions

Notes

David Ochmanek is a senior defence analyst at RAND. The views expressed here are his own and do not necessarily reflect those of RAND or the organisations that sponsor its research.

[1] Anthony H. Cordesman, *Iraq's Military Capabilities in 2002* (Washington DC: CSIS Press, 2002), pp. 2-5.

[2] See Michael R. Gordon, 'Iraq Said to Plan Tangling the U.S. in Street Fighting,' *The New York Times*, August 26, 2002, p. 1.

[3] Turkey, Kuwait, and one or two other GCC countries would be the minimum required for basing and support in this 'intermediate' option.

Chapter 3

Cake Walk, Coup or Urban Warfare: the Battle for Iraq

Toby Dodge

> 'People say to me, you [the Iraqis] are not the Vietnamese,
> you have no jungles and swamps to hide in. I reply let our
> cities be our swamps and our buildings our jungles.'[1]

Introduction[2]

Analysis of the possible responses of the Iraqi military to invasion share common assumptions and conclusions, predicting minimal opposition and a coup once the invasion has begun.[3] However, the Ba'ath Party, since seizing power in 1968, has worked hard to create a formidable military and civilian machine dedicated to securing its rule. The 'Iraqi army' as such does not exist. By building a series of competing military organisations the Ba'ath has successfully broken the collective identity of the military. Even the role of Praetorian Guard has, since the 1980s, been divided between the Republican Guard, Special Republican Guard and a myriad of quasi-military and civilian security agencies. In these circumstances, any group from within the army that wants to move against the president will find it difficult to muster a force strong enough to succeed.

The regime has used ties of family and clan to cement the upper echelons of the armed forces to the ruling elite. In addition, close association to the leadership has, over the years, tainted those charged with guarding the inner circles of government. They have been paid well for their loyalty. They have also been used to root out domestic opponents of the Ba'ath Party making them the focus of a great deal of resentment.

In these circumstances the regime's plans to combat any invasion have made a virtue out of necessity. Well-trained elite forces, those most trusted by Saddam Hussein, will form the main stay of any defence of the capital. The rest of the armed forces will be stationed in the urban conurbations that spread down the Tigris from Mosul in the north and up the Euphrates from Basra in the south. The final hope of the regime is that it will be able to inflict enough casualties to stop coalition forces before they reach Baghdad.

The Ba'athisation of the Iraqi army

Through constant purging of the officer corps and the judicious use of ideology, the Ba'ath have greatly reduced the army's ability for independent action. In any future conflict this is bound to hamper resistance. However, it will also reduce the chances of a coup. The system of intimidation and control built up over 34 years to control the army may not be broken until coalition forces reach the suburbs of Baghdad.

Since the Ba'ath Party took power it has kept the army out of politics, something all its predecessors failed to do. In the ten years before 1968 the army walked in and out of power at will, sweeping aside civilian politicians whenever they disliked what they were doing.[4] Before 1968, it was the case that 'power seems to lie around in the streets unclaimed'.[5] However, by 1980 one of the regime's fiercest academic critics would label the Ba'ath 'the most powerful and stable regime in the country's modern history'.[6]

The Ba'ath set about building the basis to its power and stability as soon as it returned to power in 1968. This meant rebuilding the army in the image of the party, thereby thoroughly curtailing its room for independent action. The Ba'ath had briefly shared power with a rough coalition of military officers between February and November 1963,[7] but had quickly became the victim of its lack of a sizable or coherent political organisation, internal divisions within its own small ranks and, ultimately, domestic rivals more powerful than itself. The lessons of its ignominious ejection from government were learnt well and have since become the hallmarks of its oversight of the military.

Immediately on return to power in 1968, and periodically ever since, the Ba'ath launched a series of purges aimed at those within the officer corps that were seen as unreliable. Since 1968, hundreds of officers have fled into exile, been prematurely retired, locked up or shot because they were perceived as disloyal or potentially so. Any leading military figure who showed the capacity for sustained independent thought and action eventually found himself sidelined, retired or worse. The route to promotion and success became political reliability not strategic vision.[8] This constant purging and reorganisation created a climate of fear sustained by the creation of a very effective security system.

Married with the re-organisation of the army was the sustained attempt to indoctrinate it. The creation of an *al-jaish al-'aqa'idi'* (the ideological army) was partly aimed at securing the allegiance of new members of the officers corps. This was achieved by imposing party discipline on the army. The military academy was now restricted to party members, with opposition activity within the army becoming a capital offence. Party commissars were placed at the head of every unit with party discipline having precedence over military orders.[9] In the long-term this indoctrination had the objective of removing from the officer corps the ideological justification for their repeated intervention into Iraqi politics. The army was no longer to be seen as the potential saviour of the nation, protecting it from the mistakes of others. That role was now to be taken by the Ba'ath Party as the vanguard of the whole Arab nation. The army was to be reduced to a tool of the Ba'ath with no ideological or practical room for independent action.[10]

The result is that today, US forces will face an army that has been thoroughly indoctrinated, with room for independent thought and action squeezed out of its officer corps. In addition, a ruthless system of surveillance and constant purges mean that soldiers have had to renounce political activity in order to survive. Throughout the 1970s and 1980s, as the army expanded, its ability to challenge the civilian politicians of the party shrank. Coup plots were continually uncovered, but their discovery pointed to the inability of mutinous officers to conspire with more than a handful of others before being betrayed.

A coup in Baghdad is certainly possible. But it only stands any chance of success when the institutions of the Ba'athist state have been severely weakened. To quote President Saddam Hussein himself: 'With our party methods, there is no chance for anyone who disagrees with us jumping into a couple of tanks and overthrowing the government. These methods have gone'.[11]

The Iraqi army in combat: 1980–91

Government control over the army has come at great cost to its military efficiency. The political logic of regime maintenance is at odds with the strategic logic of fighting another conventional army. Morale, military professionalism, esprit d'corps and the ability to act autonomously under fire have all been sacrificed to protect the government from domestic challenges. The hierarchy of military command has been continually undermined as party officials, members of the security services and civilian militias have all gained authority over the military.[12]

The beginning and progress of the 1980–88 Iran–Iraq War highlights the dominance of political logic in the use of the Iraqi army but also the pragmatism of the ruling elite when their survival is at stake. The timing and conduct of Iraq's invasion of Iran was itself a highly political act. By invading Iran at four different points along their common frontier, Saddam Hussein cast aside strategic advice in order to send a powerful political message. In its initial planning and execution the Iran–Iraq conflict was to be a 'demonstrative war', launched to show a weak Iranian leadership that they must quickly capitulate to Iraq in order to survive.[13]

Early successes in the war were quickly overtaken by a number of disastrous defeats. By 1982 the Iraqi regime, after the miscalculations of 1980, had retreated behind a set of static defences built along the border with Iran. This tactic would keep the Iraqi army under political control while halting Iranian advances by deploying technical superiority.[14] In this battle for survival it was hoped that the casualties inflicted on Iran as successive offensives were stopped would be enough to bring the war to a bloody stalemate and start negotiations.[15] As the Iranians threw more and more personnel into these attacks the regime faced an acute dilemma: it was clear that a static defence could not work on its own. But would a reformed Iraqi army, given autonomy to fight the war on its own terms, pose a greater threat to the regime than the Iranians?

To survive the war, Saddam was forced to give the army much more autonomy in order that they could make independent decisions on the basis of strategic need. The most inept senior personnel were transferred to less active roles. The influence of the political commissars attached to each unit was restricted to non-strategic issues and most importantly a 23-member National Defence Council was formed to take over operational control of the war.[16] To counterbalance this new threat Saddam greatly expanded the elite regiments of the Republican Guard, partly to act as the army vanguard, but also to protect the regime from an increasingly powerful military leadership.

The second Gulf War

This tension between the political needs of the regime and the strategic demand for an efficient army dominated the 1990–91 Gulf War. The strategically pointless Iraqi attack on the town of Khafji on 21 January 1991 can only be understood in symbolic terms. Here was the Iraqi army bravely holding out against all the odds, demonstrating to fellow soldiers and beyond them to the Iraqi population that heroic resistance was both possible and necessary.[17]

Indeed, it can be argued that the half-hearted and largely amateurish fortification of Kuwait by the Iraqis was not primarily designed to halt a coalition invasion. Instead it had a theatrical air about it. Along with Saddam Hussein's frequent references to the 'mother of all battles' the building of defences in and around Kuwait City was designed to scare the US into calling off the invasion and settling for a negotiated solution.[18]

Those military analysts who today argue that regime change in Iraq will be comparatively easy cite the 100-hour ground offensive that pushed Iraq out of Kuwait. It is true that Iraqi resistance was negligible. The troops that surrendered in their thousands to coalition forces were badly trained, poorly led and had not, in many cases, been fed for days. The Gulf War was a very one-sided affair, with the Iraqis overwhelmed by superior weaponry, technology and air power.[19]

However, it is often forgotten that the Iraqi leadership made no serious attempt to defend Kuwait City. Despite the portrayal of a heroic resistance in the 'mother of all battles', once the ground war began, Saddam Hussein quickly withdrew the majority of the Republican Guard, redeploying them around Baghdad to safeguard his regime.[20] The Iraqi leadership were well aware that the overwhelming air superiority of coalition forces would destroy their ground troops when fighting began.[21] Substandard and ill-prepared troops were left to face certain defeat. When coalition forces fought elite regiments they often faced committed soldiers who put up stiff resistance.[22]

Since the end of the Gulf War the size of the Iraqi army has been drastically reduced from 1.1 million men at its peak to less than 500,000 men.[23] The economic logic behind this is clear: sanctions have radically reduced the government's purchasing power and thus its ability to buy arms around the world. Iraq's military capacity may be as little as 20% of what it was in 1990.[24] However, there has also been an astute political logic behind this retrenchment. By shrinking the size of the army, the ruling elite has strengthened its coherence and removed all those it considered to be disloyal. The idea was to create a smaller, more disciplined force that would be ideologically committed to defending the regime. Campaigns to boost the morale of the remaining troops have been accompanied by thoroughgoing purges of the officer corps.[25]

Generalising from the stunning victory of coalition forces in 1991, removing Saddam Hussein by invading Iraq looks relatively straightforward. US and UK troops would invade, sweeping aside a demoralised, badly trained and badly equipped army with nothing to fight for. But the next time US forces encounter Iraqi soldiers, the battle will not be for a foreign land recently occupied, but for the very survival of a regime many have spent their lives serving. There is nowhere for the regime to withdraw. The fight will be for its very survival. Those troops in elite regiments such as the Republican Guard and, more importantly, the Special Republican Guard have spent their professional lives enforcing the regime's will on the rest of the population. The spontaneous outbreak of violence that heralded the end of the Gulf War in 1991 still dominates the thoughts of those closely associated with Saddam Hussein's rule. Surrounded by a hostile Iraqi population and facing a very uncertain future under a new US-backed government, the chances are that these troops as they fall back on Baghdad will fight to defend the devil they know rather than taking a chance on the mercy of a long oppressed population or invading troops.

Controlling coercion: family, clan and patronage

For over a decade Washington has looked to the Republican Guard for regime change. Today, politicians on both sides of the Atlantic still hope that a coup triggered by invasion will save them the high cost of fighting through the streets of Baghdad to reach the presidential palace. Saddam is also very aware of the dangers the Iraqi armed forces pose to his continued rule. To counter this he has successfully secured their quiescence with a judicious mix of fear, patronage and basing the hub of his regime on those tied to him by clan and family loyalties.

Those with the most sensitive job of overseeing the security services and the military are usually direct blood relatives of the president.[26] Basing the heart of the regime on close family members makes it very difficult for those at the top of the state to plot against Saddam Hussein. It is much more difficult for an individual member of his family to develop a power base independent of the president and so pose a threat to his rule. Underlying appointments of close family members is the assumption that if Saddam Hussein is removed they will also fall from power. To reinforce this message, even close family members are regularly reassigned to different jobs in the higher echelons of government to remind them that they owe their position solely to Saddam Hussein and not to any personal skills they might possess. It ensures a degree of loyalty from those who pose the largest threat to his day-to-day safety.

His younger son and heir apparent, Qusay, has long been responsible for the most important aspects of the security services and the Republican Guard. Ali Hasan al-Majid, from the al-Majid branch of the family, was responsible for pacifying the Kurds during the Iran–Iraq War. He was briefly Governor of Kuwait and most recently has been responsible for strengthening the government's position in the south of the country.

Beyond the family the basis of Saddam Hussein's long rule and the regime's power to control the armed forces is the flexible networks of patronage and resource distribution that spread out across the country from the small group of family and trusted people who surround the president. At the heart of these distribution networks is Saddam Hussein's extended clan group the al-Bu Nasir based in Tikrit and the affiliated tribes in the northwest of Iraq above Baghdad. The al-Bu Nasir and the tribes linked to them provide the social cohesion needed to run this unofficial system of regime power. The al-Bu Nasir is estimated to be no larger than 30,000 people, with affiliated tribes perhaps doubling that number.[27] Beyond them, the majority of the army's officer corps are Sunni Arabs, like the president himself. The traditional ruling class of Iraq, they are outnumbered by Shia Muslims and are well aware of the resentment this has historically caused.

The patronage-based distribution networks have been built during the 34-year rule of the regime. The nationalisation of the Iraqi Petroleum Company in 1972 and the oil price rises after 1973 gave the regime the resources to extend the networks throughout the whole of Iraqi society. Resources are channelled towards the individuals and groups that are best placed to safeguard Saddam Hussein's interests. The aim is to create a minority in Iraqi society who have a direct financial interest in the continuation of Saddam Hussein's rule.[28] The Iraqi economy has been managed primarily with the interests of these people in mind.

For patronage to work, for it to be effective in guaranteeing loyalty and obedience, it needs to exclude many more people than it benefits. Thus, the resentment of the excluded is a constant feature of all types of Iraqi politics. On a national level the Shia feel more excluded than the Sunni population. The Sunnis who are not Tikritis feel discriminated against. The Tikritis who are not from the al-Bu Nasir are resentful, as are members Saddam Hussein's family who are not in the inner circles of power. After years of benefiting from regime patronage and enforcing Saddam's rule, the recipients are more than aware of the anger and resentment that will be directed towards them if he goes. Because of this, those hoping for a coup may be very disappointed. The present regime has created a 'coalition of guilt'[29] that underpins its continued rule with corruption and great fear about what will happen when it is finally toppled.

The concentric rings of defence

An invading US army will face at least 375,000 Iraqi troops and 2,200 tanks. These numbers alone make Iraq the most effective military force in the Gulf region.[30] After the Gulf War and 11 years of sporadic bombing by US and UK planes, the Iraqi military are now used to aerial assault and are unlikely to occupy vulnerable trenches in open countryside.[31] However, analysts are right to point out that the army as a whole has suffered greatly during more than a decade of sanctions. Beyond elite regiments, equipment is old and badly maintained. Estimates suggest that the army is only 50% combat effective, and members of the regular army may well behave as they did in 1991, fleeing the battlefield once war begins.[32]

However, focusing on the size of the mainstream army, its lack of equipment and poor morale may be misleading. Saddam has surrounded himself with a robust security system spreading out from his palaces in three concentric rings. The security services become more disciplined, motivated and reliable the closer they are to the president. It is these three rings of loyal or potentially loyal people that the US will have to fight.

The Republican Guard makes up the first ring of regime security. Set up under the previous government it evolved in the 1970s into the regime's Praetorian guard. Stationed on the three main access roads to Baghdad, it is Saddam's first line of defence against a coup in the mainstream army. This parallel military force comprises 50–70,000 men, equipped with tanks and heavy armour.[33] Those serving in the Guard are better paid than ordinary soldiers and much more likely to remain loyal.[34] Many stood by their posts during the Gulf War, losing a third of their tanks.[35] They quickly rallied to Baghdad's cause in the aftermath and played the lead role in suppressing Kurdish and Shia revolts in the north and south of the country.

The Republican Guard grew rapidly in number during the Iran–Iraq War to become the striking force of the mainstream army. This growth meant that Saddam Hussein could not trust this new and sizable force. The officer corps remains the elite of the army, but as such they have developed an *esprit de corps* and sense of collective identity. Although they share Saddam Hussein's general worldview: a hatred of the United States and Israel, they have also developed an intense dislike of the president himself. Many of them blame him for strategic mistakes during the Iran–Iraq War, for the devastating war in 1990 and the subsequent isolation of Iraq.[36] For this reason they are regarded by the governing elite with a high degree of suspicion. This means it is very unlikely that the

Republican Guard and their heavy armour will, initially at least, be brought into the centre of Baghdad where they could pose a direct threat to Saddam Hussein.

The beginning of a US air campaign may well start with the targeting of the Special Republican Guard in the streets of central Baghdad.[37] This would have the added advantage of also targeting the governing elite. The Republican Guard, stationed on the outskirts of Baghdad, would then be encouraged by US propaganda to move against the government to avoid becoming the focus of bombing themselves.[38] With this in mind, it is likely that the Iraqi regime will initially deploy the Republican Guard to the south and north of the city with the primary task of slowing the advance of US troops. Only when the invading army closes in on Baghdad, leaving the regime with little choice, will the Republican Guard be brought back to defend the president.

The second ring of security protecting the regime is the Special Republican Guard, a hybrid organisation that straddles the military and security services in the tasks it performs. This group was formed in the 1980s when the Republican Guard became too large to be totally trusted.[39] This 'guard within the Guard would have received the lion's share of those Republican Guard officers with the unusual combination of competence and political reliability'.[40] They now make up the most efficient military force in Iraq, receiving the best personnel, equipment and wages available.[41] Consisting of 26,000 men and controlled by Saddam's younger son Qusay, they are the only troops with ready access to ammunition and stationed in the capital city.[42] The officers for this force are those whose loyalty to the regime is beyond doubt. It is estimated that 80% of them come from the same region of Iraq as Saddam, with their commander and senior officers hailing from Saddam's own tribe, the al-Bu Nasir.[43]

It is the Special Republican Guard that has been the regime's main tool for policing Iraqi society. Its role is so central to the regime's own survival that it was not used in the war against Iran. Instead it is a rapid intervention force, using pre-placed ammunition dumps in and around the capital, to suppress potential military coups and civilian uprisings.[44] Faced with an invasion, the fear of retribution from fellow Iraqis would be more than enough to keep them fighting for the ruling elite and the status quo. They are disciplined and motivated and could retain a strategic or even political group coherence long after the elite themselves have been killed or captured.

Finally, surrounding Saddam and the 50 or so people who rule Iraq are a myriad of competing security organisations. Each one is charged with overseeing the others, spreading an atmosphere of insecurity and mistrust throughout the whole of the security services. At the very heart of the regime the individuals responsible for the day-to-day safety of the president are all linked to him by ties of clan and family. Qusay has overall control of these organisations and this makes him the second most powerful individual in Iraq.

The two most important organisations in this final ring of protection are the Special Security Organisation, *Amn al-Khass* and the Presidential Protection Unit, the *Himayat al-Rais*. Controlled by members of Saddam's immediate family and tribe, these two groups contain highly educated and motivated individuals whose loyalty to the president is beyond doubt. They are keenly aware that their continued health and prosperity is dependent upon the rule of their boss. It is these 2,000 or so individuals who will fight to the last for the survival of the regime, using their intimate knowledge of urban Baghdad to exact as high a price as possible for regime change.

Analysts of the Iraqi military are right to point out that the army is poorly equipped, badly led and suffers from low morale. Once the US starts an air campaign they are very likely to leave their posts and return to their homes in the hope that they can avoid retribution from either side in the conflict or the larger population of Iraq. But Iraqi plans to combat the invasion implicitly recognise this fact. Opposition to US troops will not come from the conventional army and will not be situated in static defences vulnerable to attack from the air. It is the well armed and highly motivated Special Republican Guard and members of the security services, numbering as many as 30,000, that will form the defensive cordon through which invading troops will have to fight. These men are tied to the regime by clan, family and guilt. When an invasion begins they will have nowhere to go as US troops and a vengeful population threaten them equally.

Baghdad's battle plans

Faced with the overwhelming military superiority of the US army and air force, the Iraqi government has very few options in planning the defence of its country. With the reliability of the mainstream army in doubt, plans have focused on the security services, Special Republican Guard and Republican Guard. The regime also appears to have learnt from the mistakes its military made in both the Iran–Iraq War and the Gulf War.[45]

One of the main problems during the Iran–Iraq War was the army's inability to act on its own initiative. In an attempt to counter this, Baghdad has reportedly decentralised army command and control down to the lowest level possible. Responsibility for each urban centre, from Basra in the south to Mosul in the north, has been delegated to a trusted high-ranking soldier. Each town has already been garrisoned with troops, and stockpiles of weapons, fuel and food have been built up.

When hostilities start, martial law will be declared and troops brought on to the streets. In the aftermath of the Gulf War, when rebellions cut the centre of the country off from the south and the north, communications quickly broke down. By giving local control to a senior military officer, the hope is that resistance will continue even if Baghdad is cut off. The government has also set up a number of protected transmitters in an attempt to secure continued communications.

By centring its defence on urban areas, the Iraqis hope to achieve two objectives. Firstly, by moving away from static defences in open country, the Iraqi aim is to reduce if not negate the US air superiority used to such devastating effect in 1990.[46] Secondly, by drawing US troops into urban combat the aim is to slow down the advance on Baghdad, to quote Tariq Aziz, 'They are welcome to occupy our deserts for as long as they want'. The Iraqis have long held the view that US public opinion will not tolerate large numbers of American casualties and the hope is that enough US troops will be killed to force them to withdraw. Senior Iraqi politicians frequently mention the debacle in Mogadishu where the death of 18 US troops in a 15-hour fire fight led to a US withdrawal, and the suicide bombings that forced US troops to leave Beirut in 1983.

This may not just be wishful thinking. Urban warfare by its very nature favours those with local knowledge. In a war game earlier this year designed to simulate an attack on Baghdad the US military found that in spite of a six-to-one advantage they lost 100 troops in an exercise designed to oust 160 enemy fighters from urban positions.[47] The Iraqis dug in familiar surroundings will not find it difficult to inflict casualties on foreign troops. As the experience of Mogadishu in 1993 shows, US forces have limited practice of street fighting and things can quickly go wrong.[48] When faced with a small number of lightly armed but highly motivated Palestinian guerrillas, the Israelis lost 250 troops during the siege of Beirut in 1982. The resulting 10,000 mostly civilian Arab casualties gives some indication of the adverse world press campaign the US might face.[49] The Iraqi Ministry of Information has developed a highly efficient press handling system. Baghdad is already filling up with foreign media. Once bombing begins, with its inevitable civilian casualties, the hope is that international press coverage will put pressure on Washington to stop the war prematurely, much as it did in 1991.[50]

The Iraqi government clearly realises the decisive act of any attempt at regime change will be in Baghdad. It is within this sprawling city of 4.8 million that US troops will have to hunt down Saddam and his close associates. With this in mind, all troops and security services loyal to the government will, in the last instance, be massed in and around the capital.

Caught between a potentially hostile Iraqi population bent on revenge and an invading army committed to regime change, those fighting alongside Saddam will have little choice but to remain loyal to the end.[51] The result could be the worst-case scenario for US military planners: an organised, committed and disciplined force with nowhere to go, defending a highly populated urban area. In front of the world's media, US troops would have the unenviable task of distinguishing these forces from the wider innocent civilian population.

Conclusions

If the US moves towards forcible regime change in Iraq next spring, military calculations in Washington will focus on how the Iraqi army will react once coalition forces cross into Iraqi territory. But the reaction of the Iraqi armed forces is not simply a military matter. In the short-term, armed resistance to the coalition will dictate the length and nature of any military campaign. If there is significant resistance, the use of air power and long-range artillery could lead to widespread loss of civilian life and infrastructural damage. Such an outcome will affect the good will shown to any foreign forces that remain in the country after a new regime has taken power.

In the longer-term the speed and extent of an Iraqi military collapse will have profound implications for how the next government of Iraq is set up. If the US military have to fight all the way to Baghdad, then the task of post-Saddam state building will be much greater. In effect, new state institutions will have to be created and the coalition will be responsible for the maintenance of order. However, a coup triggered by international pressure on Baghdad brings with it its own problems. The sooner a coup takes place the more autonomy a new Iraqi regime will have to rule Iraq and conduct diplomacy in the way it sees fit.

Military intervention never goes exactly as its planners hope. The only thing certain about US military action in Iraq and its aftermath is that the outcome, both in the short and long term, will not be as simple or as positive as the partisan voices in Washington claim.

Notes

1 Interview by the author with Tariq Aziz, Iraqi deputy prime minister, Baghdad, Wednesday, 11 September 2002

2 I would like to thank Sue Franks of the Royal Institute of International Affairs (RIIA) library for helping with the research for this article and the Middle East Programme at RIIA for funding the research and travel. I would also like to thank Raad Alkadiri, Clare Day, Neil Partrick and Charles Tripp for their comments on an earlier draft of this paper and the participants of The International Institute for Strategic Studies Workshop, 'Iraq's Future: the immediate post-war political and social conditions'.

3 See, for example, Fouad Ajami's comment that that 'the tormented people of Iraq would be sure to erupt in joy' as soon as the US liberates them from their oppressors, in 'Iraq and the Thief of Baghdad', *New York Times*, 19 May 2002.

4 See Charles Tripp, *A History of Iraq* (Cambridge: Cambridge University Press, 2000), pp. 148–192.

5 Eliezer Be'eri, *Army officers in Arab politics and society* (London: Praeger, 1970) p. 8.

6 Samir al-Khalil, *Republic of Fear, Saddam's Iraq* (London: Hutchinson Radius, 1989), p. xviii.

7 Marin Farouk-Sluglett and Peter Sluglett, *Iraq Since 1958, From Revolution to Dictatorship* (London: I. B. Tauris, 2001), pp. 91–93.

8 See A. Abbas, 'The Iraqi Armed Forces, Past and Present', in Committee Against Repression and for Democratic Rights in Iraq, *Saddam's Iraq Revolution or Reaction?* (London: Zed Books, 1989) p. 222; and Amatzia Baram, 'The Future of Ba'athist Iraq: Power Structure, Challenges, and Prospects', Robert B. Satfoff (ed), *The Politics of Change in the Middle East*, (Boulder, CO: Westview Press, 1993).

9 See Baram, 'The Future of Ba'athist Iraq'.

10 See al-Khalil, *Republic of Fear*, p. 26.

11 See A. Abbas, 'The Iraqi Armed Forces, Past and Present', p. 222 and Samir al-Khalil, *Republic of Fear*, p. 27.

12 See Andrew Parasiliti and Sinan Antoon, 'Friends in need, foes to heed, the Iraqi military in politics', *Middle East Policy*, Vol. VII, No. 4, October 2000, p.134.

13 Shahram Chubin and Charles Tripp, *Iran and Iraq at War* (London: I.B. Tauris, 1988), pp. 54–55.

14 See John Pimlott and Stephen Badsey, *The Gulf War Assessed* (New York: Cassell, 1992), pp. 28, 30.

15 Chubin and Tripp, *Iran and Iraq at War*, p. 59.

16 Pimlott and Badsey, *The Gulf War Assessed*, p. 30.

17 See Charles Tripp, 'Symbol and Strategy: Iraq and the War for Kuwait', in Wolfgang F. Danspeckgruber with Charles R.H. Tripp (eds), *The Iraqi Aggression Against Kuwait. Strategic Lessons and Implications for Europe*, (Boulder CO: Westview Press), p. 33.

18 See Pimlott and Badsey, *The Gulf War Assessed*, p. 185.

19 See Lawrence Freedman and Efraim Karsh, *The Gulf Conflict 1990–91*, (London: Faber and Faber, 1993), p. 388.

20 Ibid, p. 402 and Dilip Hiro, *Desert*

Shield to Desert Storm: The Second Gulf War, (London: Harper Collins, 1992), p. 381.

21 J.D. McKillip, 'Iraqi Strategy during the Gulf War. An alternative viewpoint', *Military Review*, September–October, 1995, Vol. 75, No. 5, p. 48.

22 See Freedman and Karsh, *the Gulf Conflict*, p. 397.

23 Offra Bengio, 'Iraq' in Bruce Maddy-Weitzman (ed), *Middle East Contemporary Survey*, 1992, Vol. XVI, Westview Press, Boulder, p. 459.

24 See Daniel Byman, 'After the Storm, U.S. Policy Towards Iraq Since 1991', *Political Science Quarterly*, Vol. 115, No. 4, Winter 2000–01, p. 503 and David Cortright, Alistair Millar and George A. Lopez, contributing editor, Linda Gerber, Policy Brief Series, *Smart Sanctions: Restructuring UN Policy in Iraq*, Joan B. Kroc Institute and Fourth Freedom Foundation, April, 2001, p. 7.

25 See Bengio, 'Iraq', p. 459.

26 The small number of Saddam Hussein's trusted advisers that are not members of his family including Abed Hamid Mahmoud, his personal secretary, Taha Yasin Ramadhan al-Jazrawi, the vice-president, Tariq 'Aziz, the deputy prime minister and Izzat Ibrahim al-Duri, the deputy chairman of the Revolutionary Command Council.

27 See Amatzia Baram 'The Tikritis Before, During and After the War: How to Deal With Them', in this volume.

28 Estimates on the size of this group vary. Baram judges it to be one million of Iraq's 23 million people whereas Tripp puts the figure at 500,000. See Amatzia

Baram, 'Between Impediment and Advantage: Saddam's Iraq', United States Institute of Peace Special Report, Washington, June 1998, p. 13 and Tripp, *A History of Iraq*, p. 264.

29 I would like to thank Charles Tripp for suggesting this term.

30 See Anthony H. Cordesman, 'If We Fight Iraq: Iraq and The Conventional Military Balance', Centre for Strategic and International Studies, 27 February 2002, p. 1.

31 Michael O'Hanlon, *The Wall Street Journal*, 29 May 2002

32 See *The Military Balance 2002–2003*, International Institute for Strategic Studies, (Oxford: Oxford University Press, 2002).

33 See Brian Whitaker, 'Loyalty of Iraq's elite in doubt', *The Guardian*, 20 September 2002, and Baram, 'The Tikritis Before, During and After the war: Positions in Saddam's Power Structure, Options and now to Deal With Them'.

34 Amatzia Baram, 'The Future of Ba'athist Iraq: Power Structure, Challenges, and Prospects,' p. 35.

35 Ibid., p. 36.

36 This is based on interviews carried out by the author in the Persian Gulf region in 1999 with senior Iraqi military figures who had recently left Baghdad.

37 The Special Republican Guard were one of the main targets of the Anglo–American *Operation Desert Fox* in December 1998.

38 See Toby Dodge 'Iraq and the "Bush Doctrine"', *The World Today*, Vol. 58, No. 4, April 2002, p. 6.

39 See Pimlott and Badsey, *The Gulf War Assessed*, p. 179.

40 Ibid.

41 Sean Boyne, 'Inside Iraq's security network', *Janes*

Intelligence Review, July 1997, p. 313.

[42] See Mustafa Alani, 'Saddam's Support Structure', McKnight, Partrick & Toase (eds), *Gulf Security: Opportunities and Challenges for the New Generation*, Royal United Services Institute, London, 2001 and the Economist Intelligence Unit, *Iraq Country Report*, Iraq, 1997.

[43] Baram, 'The Tikritis Before, During and After the war'.

[44] See Alani, 'Saddam's Support Structure'.

[45] Interview by the author with Tariq Aziz, deputy prime minister Baghdad, Wednesday 11 September 2002.

[46] Interview with Tariq Aziz.

[47] See Scott Peterson, 'Iraq Prepares for Urban warfare', *The Christian Science Monitor*, 4 October 2002.

[48] See Mark Odell and Peter Spiegel, 'Iraq war would bring bloody street fighting, *Financial Times*, 18 October 2002.

[49] Paul Rogers, 'The coming war over Iraq: prelude, course, aftermath', 14 August 2002, Global Security, http://www.opendemocrasy.net/.

[50] For the skills of Iraqi press handlers see Franklin Foer, 'How Saddam manipulates the US Media', *The New Republic*, 28 October 2002.

[51] It is estimated that as much as 60-75% of Baghdad's population is Shia along with 10% Kurd. See Baram, 'Between Impediment and Advantage: Saddam's Iraq', p. 5.

Chapter 4

A Few Days After: State and Society in a post-Saddam Iraq

Isam al Khafaji

One minor casualty of military-driven regime change will be the huge edifice of analysis, speculation and projection on the assumed heterogeneity and artificiality of Iraqi society, the imminent Sunni–Shia civil war and the eventual dismemberment of Iraq. Such speculation, often cast as statements of fact, has flourished over the decade following the Gulf War. This conventional wisdom superceded another set of statements that prevailed in the 1980s. Then, Iraq was conceived as an allegedly modernist and secular Ba'athist regime facing an obscurantist Iran.

Rejecting these statements, however, does not mean subscribing to the rosy and self-deceptive scenario often adopted by an Iraqi opposition in exile. This has tended to reduce the structural crises of Iraqi society to one man, Saddam Hussein: a tyrant who has managed to stay in power for more than three of the eight decades of the modern Iraqi state by brutalising his opponents and the population at large.

Neither the apocalyptic scenario of Iraqi sects, nationalities or tribes at war with each other, nor the rosy vision of a harmonious people going back to life as usual once the tyranny is overthrown, is likely to materialise in the immediate aftermath of regime change. Instead we have to assess the more realistic social outcomes as the dust of the battle settles. What social variables would be at play? What constants – if any – could force themselves on a new ruling elite and therefore preserve elements of continuity in the functioning and structures of the Iraqi state and society? These questions, by their very nature, may be easier to address in a longer-term perspective in which one can analyse the impact of the disposal of oil-revenues by the state on the various social actors. In the short-term, however, one has to look at the likely structural changes that would be introduced, irrespective of the specific form of regime change.

This is a very arduous task, given the fact that how regime change would be realised depends to a large degree on the specific military strategy adopted by the US in the war against Saddam, the outcome of the internal struggles within the American administration between the 'realists' and the 'neo-conservatives', and the possible responses of the Iraqi population to US military strikes.

Atomisation, identity and collective action

The legacy of 34 years of monolithic rule and 54 years of republican regimes, whose sole legitimacy rested on self-designed interim constitutions and the recognition of the international community, will have a powerful impact on the immediate post-Saddam political setting. This is true whether one believes the premise that the vast majority of Iraqis are opposed to the existing Ba'ath regime, or whether they would merely prefer a change in the ruling junta without changing the basic parameters of the Ba'athist system. This legacy will unfold as political opponents of the existing regime try to build their internal constituencies among segments of a population whose political, judicial and constitutional culture has been drastically impoverished over previous decades.

The horrendous task of overthrowing Saddam's regime may prove to be less painful than that of dealing with the interest groups that have taken firm root in Iraqi society and owe varying forms and degrees of allegiance to the power structure that has been in place since 1968. These interest groups range from networks of special intelligence operatives, armed militias and other irregulars, networks of Ba'ath party apparatchiks and contractors, profiteers and influence brokers. Their allegiance to the Ba'athist power structure ranges from family ties, tribal alliances and ideological commitment to the basic tenets of Ba'athism, to a mere show of loyalty to Saddam Hussein or sheer opportunism. Whatever the intentions of these new power blocs an accommodation with some of these interest groups would have to be sought, at least in the short term. But how would non-organised Iraqis – that is, the majority of the population – react to this evolving situation?

Stereotyped visions of Iraqi society have yielded the now familiar picture of a country cleanly cut into a Kurdish north, Sunni centre and Shia south. From this picture follows a simple arithmetic approach to understanding identities: the Kurds are bound by ethnic ties while the Sunni and Shia blocs are cemented by tribal/sectarian ones. This type of bloc identification takes a further step by assuming that, unlike the Shia, Sunnis are sympathetic to Ba'athism, or to some variant of pan-Arab nationalism, while the Shia loyalties are to fundamental Islamic parties. Politico-religious identities among Sunnis and Shia are assumed to pass through the local tribal chiefs of each community.

The advocates of primordialising Iraqi society rarely provide any evidence to substantiate their theses. The fact that Saddam's regime relies heavily on tribal solidarity in cementing its cohesion is taken as sufficient proof. Yet, while the Ba'athist regime has striven to revive tribal politics, especially since the end of the Gulf War, its reception within society has been half-hearted and its success far from obvious.

Iraq's primordialisers overlook the fact that the Ba'athist regime left to its own devices and given sufficient resources would not have encouraged any form of collective solidarity among the population. Such collective solidarities have played a part in organising the ruling elite, but were certainly not meant to apply to the entire society. In fact, the success of Ba'athism in subjugating the Iraqi people to its rule for a relatively long period lies precisely in its ability to atomise the population and link each individual vertically to the patron-state. The process of atomisation, it should be stressed, was not solely a product of this, or any other regime's policies. It has its basis in the rentier structure of the Iraqi economy, which made it possible for the state to carry out extensive welfare programmes, without in the meantime, appearing to be indebted to the population through the ordinary process of resource extraction via taxation.

While the rentier structure made it possible for authoritarianism to survive and gain acquiescence among large sections of the population, it must be emphasised that the tenacity of the rentier nature of society and the economy were by no means the product of 'natural' or 'objective' forces. Ba'athist policies played a tremendous role in perpetuating this state of affairs by discouraging any search for efficient and alternative sources of income and thus kept the population dependent on the state and its oil revenues, such that on the eve of the Iran–Iraq war, oil alone accounted for around 60% of Iraq's GDP.

The state monopolised these tremendous oil revenues and became the biggest single employer and purchaser in the economy. This situation, unlike Soviet-type economies, did encourage the rise of affluent private business groups. Yet even private business was almost entirely dependent on the state and had a powerful stake in preserving a highly secretive and corrupt system that allowed it unfettered access to the lucrative resources of the state. Thus the general atmosphere of relative abundance allowed the Iraqi regime to propagate the illusion of a corporatist and non-antagonistic society in which the state embodied the interests of all Iraq's citizens. In this respect, the Ba'ath Party and its front organisations, which were the only legal ones, were designed to act as a control mechanism, spreading their tentacles to the farthest reaches of the country.

Only after the 1991 popular uprising and the crushing defeat of the Gulf War did Saddam Hussein make a reluctant admission that intermediate social layers between the state and individuals were required to extend control mechanisms and channel people's frustrations and demands. The Ba'ath Party's own ability to do this had proven to be an abject failure.

But tribalism has not proved to be an effective binding mechanism for the various segments of Iraqi society. Firstly, the mere fact that the use of tribal title is forbidden by the Revolutionary Command Council to hide the dominance of Saddam Hussein's tribe is evidence that the ruling regime finds it difficult to convince ordinary people of the merits of reliance on kinship relations. Secondly, even within the power elite, kinship relations have been used to solidify interest groups and not express more generalised social relations. The brutal murder of Saddam Hussein's sons-in-law in 1996 and the subsequent assassinations, disappearances and imprisonment of numerous relatives who did not comply with the leader's will shows that kinship is a means to cement interest groups, even a powerful one, but is not the basis of those groups themselves. The third – and perhaps most important – indicator that tribalism is not effective in forging loyalties in Iraq is the course of the 1991 uprising and the mobilising dynamics it unleashed.

It is widely accepted that the uprising was a predominantly urban phenomenon. This is not only due to the fact that the urban population accounts for 72% of the total population of Iraq. Oil rentierism had marginalised the rural population to such an extent that a strategy of cutting off the countryside, or provincial towns from the major cities, especially the capital – the essence of peasant guerilla warfare – would have punished the rural 'liberated' areas rather than the encircled cities. Under these circumstances it was natural that the now extensive accounts on the 1991 *intifada* hardly mention any role for entire tribes acting in unison or of recourse to tribal sentiments in order to mobilise the population for, or against, the *intifada*.

Even today, with Saddam Hussein's regime encouraging tribal chiefs to act as a buffer between the leadership and ordinary individuals, in rural areas and in the squatter districts of new migrants to cities, the chiefs and their supposed tribe-members use the new policy in a very pragmatic way – one which does not signify a genuine sense of solidarity.

While the argument against widespread tribal solidarity among Iraqis can be convincingly made, this is not the case for national Kurdish sentiments or the Shia sense of grievance and discrimination. Yet, here again the picture is much more complicated than the primordialisers of Iraqi society would believe. The 1991 *intifadha*, as one of the rare spontaneous collective actions in the modern history of Iraq, can serve as a testing ground for this conclusion.

In Kurdistan, the unfulfilled national aspirations for statehood and self-rule have made it possible for the two historically entrenched political parties, the Kurdistan Democratic Party and the Patriotic Union of Kurdistan, to articulate religious, tribal and local solidarity in a rare show of national unity under the leadership of modern party structures. In several areas, Dohuk for example, the pro-Saddam mercenary troops – the Jaish, as the Kurds call them – changed sides and sparked the revolt out of sheer opportunism. The Jaish, however, were eventually absorbed in one of the two major parties. The regional historical cleavage within Iraqi Kurdistan between Bahdinan, the more prosperous, pacifist and less culturally assertive western part and Suran, the poorer more militant and culturally sophisticated eastern part, as well as the historical difference within Suran between the two major urban centers, Arbil and Sulaymaniyah, partially account for the weight of each of the two major parties in different regions and in consequence, the subsequent *de facto* division into two semi-autonomous regions, each under the control of one of these parties.

How did Shia identity manifest itself in the southern and central parts of Iraq which, alongside Kurdistan, were swept by the 1991 revolt? Can one deduce the Shi'ite nature of the revolt by referring to its geography? And if so, can we assume the existence of a unifying Shi'ite sense of identity? It is a fact that the predominantly Sunni governorates of Nineveh (Mosul), Anbar (Dulaim) (and Diyala) did not witness widespread protests during the *intifada*, but that also applies to the predominantly Shia governorates along the Tigris (Wasit and to a lesser degree Maisan). Many indicators of Sunni dissent were apparent and sparked the revolt in the Sunni city of Zubair, south of Basra. In several important towns, such as Hilla, dissident Ba'athist officers played a leading role in the *intifada*. The paramount sheikh of the powerful Sunni Shammar tribe moved to Syria in a discrete attempt to coordinate a joint anti-Saddam action with the Syrians.

Participation in the revolt was not just determined by the degree of opposition to the Ba'athist regime in different areas of the country. Geopolitical factors, such as the level of state control and geographical proximity to Baghdad, and the immediate impact of the war's devastation on various regions may partly explain why, for example, a city like Mosul that is not known for its sympathy with the Ba'athist regime, did not revolt or why Baghdadis could not unite to launch a fatal blow against the regime.

The fact that the rebellion took place in predominantly Shia regions does not mean that the Shia acted in unison. They constitute the single largest confessional community in Iraq, but were dispersed over the whole political spectrum, from individuals occupying leading posts in the Ba'athist governing machinery, to liberals, monarchists and communists. Those Shia who maintained a religious posture, or opposed the regime because of its anti-Shia stance, also showed a wide array of loyalties. The vast majority followed the Supreme Mujtahid, whose teachings leaned towards non-interference in party politics. As for the fewer partisan Islamists, their organisations reflected regional loyalties more than ideological differences. Hence, the Organisation of Islamic Action was dominated by ulama from Kerbala, the Movements of Mujahideen by ulama from Kadhimiyya and Da'wa by Najafis, while the Supreme Council tried to uphold the façade of an umbrella group for all the Islamist organisations.

While there is a quasi-unanimity regarding the under-representation of Shias in state agencies and political institutions (but with radically diverse explanations for this situation), very few, if any, common themes and objectives could cement a unity among Iraqi Shia, who number more than 12 million. A widespread hatred of the Ba'athist regime and a loose sense of the injustices done to the Shia and Kurds, as well as many others, can translate into an infinite array of protest movements among an atomised population.

Unleashing the genie

While no one can forecast with any degree of certainty the specific form of alignments among the various segments of the population in the immediate aftermath of an American assault, mass actions encapsulating a volatile mixture of euphoria, anxiety about the future, attempts to redress the grave injustices of more than three decades of tyranny and the joy of practicing freedom would almost certainly be the order of the day once the people firmly believed that Saddam's days were numbered.

Where could the violence come from? Not from an imagined 'vertical' civil war pitting Shi'ites against Sunnis, or Arabs against Kurds, but from the source that has been contaminating and corrupting Iraqi society over the past four decades: the highly politicised and violent social atmosphere created by the Ba'athist regime. A protest movement against the carnage of war and the humiliation of a defeated army can quickly turn to targeting the most visible symbols of authority – known collaborators, members of the numerous organs of oppression and control – or, simply, attacking people hailing from Tikrit. In the latter case, revenge need not necessarily take a sectarian meaning. Sunni regions relegated to a secondary position under the Ba'ath, such as Samarra and Dulaim, may well show signs of hatred that surpass those of the Shia sections of society.

Whatever the degree of resistance, or lack of it, that the Special Republican and Republican Guards, the regular armed forces, the intelligence, security and party members show an invading US-led force, it is reasonable to assume that many members of the security apparatuses – in addition to a host of other government organisations such as the popular army, Saddam's Fedayeen, or the Iranian Mujahideen e-Khalq – would keep their arms, whatever attempts were made to demilitarise the population. As new political organisations emerge and organisations in exile re-establish themselves inside Iraq, they will vie to recruit many of these demobilised elements in order to impose themselves by force in the new political atmosphere.

The ensuing scene may not look as chaotic as the civil wars in Afghanistan or Lebanon, but it will entail a degree of violence even if a US or multilateral occupation force or a hastily reformed army tries to impose order. Newly formed organisations would be tempted to recruit armed individuals because they would be faced with a power vacuum in which many already armed groups would try to impose their authority on the rest of society. The Supreme Council of the Islamic Revolution (SCIRI) claims that its Badr Corps has 10,000 men-under-arms. The two main Kurdish parties have several thousand *peshmergas* in the process of being transformed into a regular Kurdish army. Moreover, the US Department of State is inclined to deal with these factions as essential elements in preserving order in a transitional Iraq, thus legitimising their existence.

One possible scenario is that disbanded armed units or individuals from the Ba'athist regime would search for protection and empowerment by joining one of the newly organised parties. But unlike the post-1991 situation in Kurdistan where the two major parties competed – and succeeded – in recruiting the chiefs of tribes that had collaborated with Saddam Hussein, the Baghdad-based organisations of a post-Saddam era would not have as much appeal as these disbanded Ba'athist units. Because both Kurdish parties adopted a general national liberation agenda, Kurdish Jaish tribes made their decisions to join one of the parties mainly along tribal/ regional criteria; namely, which party was more influential in the locality of the tribe, the political allegiance of rival tribes and tribal/ regional connections with a leader of one of the parties.

Assuming that the active parties in the immediate post-Saddam era would be the same ones that are in existence today, the obvious option for the ex-Saddam militias would be to join, or to show allegiance, to those organisations whose outlook, composition and leadership background is closest to their own: the Iraqi National Accord (INA) – an organisation composed of ex-Ba'athists calling for a limited *coup d'ètat*. One can understand then why the Iraqi National Congress (INC), an organisation with a strongly liberal and pro-Western agenda, has been lobbying the US administration to train thousands of Iraqi expatriates under the pretext of creating a force to preserve order in the post-Saddam era. For short of outright backing by any occupation force, a liberal, pro-Western agenda has little chance of ruling by ballot in the immediate post-Saddam era. Moreover, it is highly unlikely that the Iraqi supporters of such an agenda in exile would be enthusiastic to return 'home' to boost the INC's political standing. Hence, only a well-trained armed militia can serve as a means for securing a share of power for the INC.

A US/multilateral occupation force can do little to impose order in the short term. For, despite a probable euphoric mood among the Iraqis sparked by being rid of Saddam's tyranny and the probability of a beneficent occupation, an Islamic militia supported by its ex-enemies, the nationalist remnants of the Ba'ath, could play on an apprehensive mood to wage a 'war of liberation' against the imperialist infidels.

Guarding the guardians

The first order of the day in a post-Saddam era is to control the inevitable cycle of violence and retribution which could easily degenerate into long, drawn-out civil strife, but not outright civil war. Another major source of violence could be the struggle to control the oil-rich governorate of Kirkuk. This issue is of particular historical importance since it was at the root of the collapse of the 1970 autonomy agreement between the Kurds and the central government in Baghdad.

A possible worst-case scenario may include not just the Kurds fighting Turkomans, and eventually Turkey, but also an inter-Kurdish civil war. Kirkuk is geographically closer to the area that Jalal Talabani controls, and its Kurdish inhabitants are generally more receptive to his PUK than to Barzani's KDP. What if the former decides to strike a deal with the Turkomans at the expense of his Kurdish rival in order to get out of the confines of his isolation in Sulaymaniyah and to strongly enhance his bargaining power? The logical response by Barzani would be to enter into an alliance with the Arab tribes whom Saddam had settled in the region. Such a scenario could undermine the stability of post-conflict Iraq and pave the way for an authoritarian regime under the pretext of preserving national unity.

Rapid occupation of Kirkuk by US or other international forces may infuriate the two Kurdish parties who would interpret this move as appeasement of the Turks and another chapter of betrayal in the history of US-Kurdish relations. This perception might be accurate in so far as the United States's relations with Turkey are as strategically important as ever: Turkey is the sole point from which the US can deploy ground forces into northern Iraq. Neither the US nor a future pro-American Iraqi administration would deem alienation of Kurds to be a problem. Once Saddam is overthrown, the Kurds are likely to lose their special status in US policy towards Iraq. It remains to be seen whether a US claim that its occupation has spared Iraq a Turkish invasion could appease a population that had not been ruled by a foreign power since the 1930s.

Even if the US could legitimise its military presence in Iraq, it would be much more difficult to impose order on society. In fact, US troops may prove to be an additional burden for security if a section of the Iraqi population decides to wage a 'war of liberation' against a foreign presence. This would be especially difficult to counter, as Iraq is an urbanised country with three of its major cities having a population of more than a million each. The question of who would be in charge of security has already become a highly charged issue within the US government and among the Iraqi opposition affiliated with the US. This is because the spectrum of views in Washington on the future role of Iraq within the US's global strategy has a direct bearing on the kind of a leadership and political system for Iraq that the US will favour.

The dispute between two views of US aims and interests, one broadly defined as 'idealist' and one 'realist' is not a new one. However, under the present US administration, the dispute has been institutionalised, with the Department of State and the CIA broadly associated with a so-called 'realist' stance. This perceives that a change at the head of the regime in Baghdad is a more or less the final step towards restoring stability to a region disturbed by Saddam Hussein. US interests would be best served by a limited change that entailed the removal of Saddam and his close associates while leaving the basic institutions of Saddam's regime intact. After this a façade of parliamentary democracy resembling the Egyptian one could be created; a 'leading' party composed of 'reformed' ex-Ba'athists would remain along with a strong authoritarian president backed by a restrained army and intelligence service.

At the other end of the spectrum are the 'idealists'. This group consists of the civilian leadership at the Pentagon, backed by many in Congress and the office of the vice-president and possibly the National Security Council. For this group, regime change in Iraq would be the beginning of a 'democratic wave'. This would eventually transform Iraq into a pro-American liberal oasis spearheading the democratic transformation of the whole the region.

The history of this dispute in Washington goes back to at least the mid-1980s, when an influential segment within the Reagan and Bush administrations, supported by a battery of 'scholars', propagandists, businessmen and politicians, invested a great deal of effort and resources in cultivating the idea of bringing nationalist dictatorships, especially that of Saddam Hussein, into close alliance with the US, to combat fundamentalism and ensure a stable supply of oil to the West.

This line of reasoning never lost its influence even when Saddam turned into a major threat to the US interests in 1990. However, with the Iraqi defeat in the second Gulf War and the eruption of a popular revolt that swept Iraq from north to south, there were calls for a radical change of regime in Iraq. This was especially the case after President G.W.H. Bush's call for the Iraqi army and the people to 'take matters into their hands'. Yet, the ex-advocates of alliance with Saddam Hussein were still in a position to play a crucial role in convincing the administration not to support the 1991 *intifada* and to stand by as Saddam's troops butchered no less than 60,000 victims while allied forces occupied one-sixth of Iraqi territory. The conservative argument of these advisers was that a popular revolt would bring unwanted consequences.

Over the past decade, these two policy approaches found their counterparts amongst the Iraqi opposition. The US realists focused on the INA, while the neo-conservatives at the Pentagon backed the INC. Yet it would be an oversimplification to label these organisations, as well as other less important factions and individuals, mere agents of an American agenda. The composition of each of these organisations reflects, to a large extent, the deep changes in society introduced by the Ba'athist regime. The INC is mainly composed of individuals who owe their social, economic or political rise to the pre-republican regimes prior to 1958, while the INA's leadership belongs to the strata that rose with the republican regimes, especially under the Ba'ath. Hence, the leaders of the INC have nothing in common with the existing elite and view the prevailing authoritarian norms with hostility, while the INA leadership broke from the Ba'ath for various reasons, but still share many of the tendencies and approaches, to which they owe their social, economic and political standing.

The Tunisian syndrome

How would these two approaches, within the US administration as well as within the Iraqi opposition, shape a hypothetical post-Saddam landscape? How Saddam's regime finally falls will shape, to a large degree, the immediate reactions of ordinary Iraqis and how they overcome its awesome legacy.

There are four broad scenarios for how regime change may or may not take place. The first, and least likely, would involve a series of devastating US military attacks on the infrastructure and civilian population (Washington has more or less ruled out attacks on non-military infrastructure). This would allow Ba'athist propaganda to portray the war as targeting the Iraqi people and Saddam Hussein as the defender of national interests. A second scenario would involve Saddam Hussein's total capitulation over weapons of mass destruction. This would presuppose his ultimate goal is to cling to power at any price. The third scenario would be an army general delivering the silver bullet. Finally, a popular revolt would force the regime to surrender. These four possible outcomes will determine how euphoric or despondent ordinary Iraqis will be, along with how much they will trust the new regime, and therefore whether they will try to take justice to the streets or leave it for the new regime to administer.

How can a transitional administration enforce its will on the population? Even if the armed forces show no signs of resistance to regime change their loyalty to the new regime cannot be taken for granted. More than 30 years of indoctrination and isolation from the outside world would render communication between the new administration and the armed forces a very hard task. The sudden collapse of the Ba'athist regime of terror would present a golden opportunity to lose discipline without fear of reprisal. But the most worrying aspect is the vast networks of kin and family interests that would keep the administration in a nightmarish state of alert for fear of coup attempts.

Discussions among the opposition groups in exile on how to deal with such a situation reveal some interesting trends. Advocates of 'regime change lite', start from what they see as 'Iraq's cultural norms and existing structures'. Iraq's turbulent history and regional setting, as well as an awesome Ba'athist legacy, do not allow for the luxury of planning a democratic transformation in the short or even medium term. Priority should be given to stability and a minimum of normality. On the face of it, this approach seems to keep interference in the country's internal affairs to a minimum. Its thrust, however, is reminiscent of the British colonial policies of the 1920s. Tribal chiefs would be given a big say in Iraq's domestic policies, and SCIRI's militias would be deployed to maintain order in the south. In the meantime, and under the pretext of preserving stability, the main structures of the Ba'athist regime and many of its leaders are to be kept in place in the post-Saddam system.

By contrast, INC analysis is based on a different set of assumptions. For them the Ba'athist system is comparable to the Nazi regime. Their starting point, therefore, is a process of de-Ba'athification, which would entail the dismantling of the basic structures of Saddam's regime, a heavy reliance on US assistance and a long-term presence in Iraq in order to preserve order and restructure the political system. A militia of Iraqis previously in exile would then be created to form the nucleus of a future armed force.

A closer look at both scenarios reveals that they would tend to create political facts with long-term repercussions for Iraqi society.

The 'regime change lite' scenario not only reproduces much of the tenets of the Ba'athist regime, thus threatening to empty the process of change of its profound reformative agenda, but it also involves the reinvigoration and imposition of defunct social and political structures under the pretext of taking the local factors into consideration.

The 'idealistic' scenario, on the other hand, is based on the premise that a fully democratic agenda, or laying the grounds for a democratic transition in Iraq, cannot be the product of the 'internal' functioning of Iraqi society itself. It would, therefore, require a sustained and intensive American military occupation for a relatively long period of time. The occupation and transformation of Japan into a democratic state is the model for this approach.

Historical experience, however, shows that social structures follow their own patterns of transformation. A progressive leadership or a status-quo orientated or foreign power may try to impose their political agendas under the rubric of modernisation or respect for indigenous cultures, but the logic of social structures eventually prevails by inflicting its revenge from those who attempt to ignore them. Armed militias – whether belonging to SCIRI or to the INC – tend to create their own interests, do not reflect popular wishes, and are not perceived by the population as fulfilling a function on their behalf. In fact, militias tend to usurp power, terrorise the population and boost the power base of their patrons rather than act as a nucleus for truly *national* armed forces. In a country that has been depleted of legal structures and representative traditions, such armed militias will only distort the long-anticipated electoral process and will prove very hard to integrate into the body politic.

Only reconstituted Iraqi armed forces and the institutions of law enforcement can impose authority and order. Even in these circumstances, the imposition of order would be carried out with great difficulty in the immediate wake of regime change. Apart from the technical problems involved in the rehabilitation of what would be defeated and devastated armed forces, there is the more daunting task of transforming them from a politicised and oppressive force into a national institution recognised by the population as a defender of order and sovereignty.

The regular armed and police forces can invoke a history of marginalisation and humiliation under the Ba'athist regime to gain sympathy among the population. Unlike the special elite forces – the Republican Guard and later, the Special Republican Guard and the various intelligence and security apparatuses – the armed and police forces can regain some degree of respectability among the population. By the end of the Iran–Iraq War, the privileges that had been heaped upon the regular officers began to dry up and generals who had a positive record were demoted or punished. The minister of defence was killed in a helicopter accident widely thought to be a murderous act of Saddam Hussein. To perform their duties, however, the regular armed forces need to be seen as an institution of a legitimate state.

Legitimacy in contemporary Iraq, it should be remembered, has rarely been established through a democratically adopted constitution that various state agencies vie to respect and protect. Rather, it has been mostly acquired through the patron role of the state: by the state rendering services to significant segments of the population in return for loyalty. The fact that the first republican regime of 1958 promulgated an interim constitution was not a major issue in the debates among its supporters or adversaries as long as the regime was seen as fulfilling national goals. The same applies to the Ba'athist regime, which has survived for 34 years without a permanent constitution.

A first step towards legitimising a post-Saddam regime is by international recognition and membership of international organisations. But this is hardly sufficient to induce recognition by Iraqi society itself. It is within society that the delicate balance should be struck between representatives of the population who can command a degree of respectability and credibility on their own moral and political merits, and leaders who can command the loyalty of the armed and law enforcement agencies. Striking such a balance could prove to be tremendously difficult, given the fact that at times of revolutionary upheaval, expectations among the people tend to be high and credibility would rise proportionately with the distance an individual or organisation was from the defunct regime. On the other hand, however, these distant individuals, who would by definition be those who had not been involved in running the state, would mostly be alien to the institutions and apparatuses running the country.

Short of a full-scale revolution that would produce its own alternative leadership and institutions, an unstable and conflictual interregnum will characterise the period following the fall of the regime. While a spontaneous revolt is a likely possibility in the aftermath – or even before – a military attack on Iraq, the atomisation and impoverishment of Iraq's political culture would make it almost impossible for this to develop into a full-scale revolution. More than a decade of devastating sanctions and three decades of tyranny have taken a heavy toll on the educated middle classes from which an enlightened alternative leadership could emerge. It should be no surprise if, after decades of untold suffering by millions of Iraqis, some of the old butchers may return to champion the new fashionable causes of liberalism, a free market and pro-Americanism.

Chapter 5

Saddam's Power Structure: the Tikritis Before, During and After the War

Amatzia Baram

Origins

Economic and social factors dominated the selection of the first generation of Iraqi army officers. They tended to hail from Baghdad and Mosul. They started their careers at the military school in Baghdad established in 1870 by the Ottoman governor Midhat Pasha. To be able to attend the school, which was free of charge, a child either needed to have family in the city where he could stay overnight, or his parents had to pay for his upkeep if they lived outside of Baghdad. The child also had to have a good basic education before he entered the military school. Families from the small provincial towns could not afford these expenses. The result was that when Iraq became a state in 1920, the available reservoir of officers, people who had served in the middle to upper ranks of the Ottoman army, came mainly from the middle classes of Baghdad and Mosul. The majority of the population of Basra could not join the Ottoman officer corps because they were Shia.

In the aftermath of the collapse of the Ottoman Empire (under King Faisal I 1921–33), some officers remained in the armed forces, while others retired or turned to politics. They came to be known as the Sharifian officers, because they served the Sharifi Hashemite royal family which King Faisal I represented. These officers belonged to two very different groups. One consisted of officers who defected from the Ottoman army during the First World War to join the rebellious army of King Faisal's father, Sharif Hussein of Mecca, as well as officers who had been captured by the British and were offered the choice of fighting with the rebels or remaining in prison. Most of them chose release. Almost all these officers, who had fought alongside Faisal against the Ottomans, remained loyal to him and to the British, throughout their military and political careers. The Iraqi officers who fought in the Ottoman army against the British until the bitter end, were an entirely different group. Even though they eventually joined the administration of the new king in Baghdad, they remained a reservoir from which the most bitter enemies of the Hashemite monarchy and the British emerged. Very few members of either group came from the countryside.

The transformation of Iraq's economy and society that began in the 1930s brought about important changes in the composition of the officer corps. Young men from small towns in the Sunni–Arab triangle (Baghdad–Mosul–Jazira), and above all, from Tikrit, started to permeate the officer corps. There were two reasons for this: Tikrit's main industry, the *kalak*, a small boat made of animal skins, had become obsolete. The young generation that had depended on the *kalak* industry were now looking for new economic opportunities. Many went to Baghdad's teaching college, while others chose military service. Some, such as Saddam Hussein's maternal uncle and childhood friend, Ahmad Hasan al-Bakr, who later became the president of Iraq, first became teachers and then army officers, which promised greater social status in the young Iraqi state than school teaching.

The other reason behind the massive penetration of young Tikritis into the officer's corps was the influence of Mawlud Mukhlis. Mukhlis's family came from the town of Haditha on the Euphrates, west of Baghdad. They moved to Mosul, and then to Tikrit, and acquired a great deal of land. Mukhlis was one of the officers who served under Faisal in the Arab revolt and then came with him to Baghdad. During the first two decades of the monarchy he achieved prominence and used his political influence to help young Tikritis join the military academy. As a result, when the monarchy was toppled by the military, Tikritis were already well established as middle-ranking officers in the Iraqi armed forces.

When the Ba'ath Party came to power for the second time in July 1968 (they had come to power first in 1963, but only for nine months), they purged the officers' corps of 'disloyal elements', including Nasserites, pro-Syrian Ba'athists and leftists suspected of Communist inclinations. A very high percentage of those who were not considered disloyal were Tikriti.

Over the years, in a slow and almost imperceptible process, Tikritis have enjoyed increasingly preferential treatment in the armed forces. With some important exceptions, they were promoted faster than most of their colleagues. In their quest for regime security, Saddam Hussein and his maternal cousin Adnan Khayr Allah Talfah, who became Minister of Defence in 1977, preferred a mediocre but loyal officer to an excellent officer whose loyalty was questionable. Many of these Tikritis were also members of Saddam Hussein's tribe, the Albu-Nasir, easily identified by their surname, al-Nasiri. This eventually limited the army's performance on the battlefield, but reduced the chances of a military *coup d'état*.

Another career that attracted Tikritis in large numbers was working for the internal security services. According to an interview with an Iraqi expatriate in the West, who was a member of the party elite during the first years of Ba'ath rule in Baghdad, President Bakr, a Tikriti and member of the Albu-Nasir, was approached by his friend, Saddam's uncle Khayr Allah Talfah, who suggested that the president ought to rely on Saddam to build a protective ring around himself. Khayr Allah Talfah argued that party loyalty had proved insufficient in 1963 when the Ba'ath lost power, and so there was a need to rely on family ties to cement President Bakr's grip on power. According to other sources, the job was in fact offered to a few party luminaries but they turned it down: no other senior leader in the party was ready to assume the job of security chief. This was regarded as an inferior and brutal job. Saddam, however, was glad to oblige.

Whatever the case, the result was that Saddam became the czar of internal security very soon after the Ba'ath regime came to power. One of his first acts was to establish a presidential protection force – the Himaya – based on young Tikritis, mainly from his own tribe. Brought in at age 15 or 16 they were trained in the presidential compound in Baghdad for about three years. These young men composed the most immediate protection ring around President

Bakr while turning him into a *de facto* prisoner. The young men owed Saddam everything – their position, their possessions, their arranged marriages, and their social status. They were looked after. In exchange, they offered total loyalty and submitted to strict discipline. They feared and admired Saddam, whom they dubbed 'Ammna al-Chebir' ('Our Great Uncle').

During his time as vice-president (November 1969–July 1979), Saddam also flooded the internal security apparatuses at all levels with his tribesmen and other loyalists, mostly from the towns of Tikrit, al-Dur, Beiji and Uja. Tikrit is not a large town and its human resources are limited, but if placed in the right positions, relatively few loyalists could make a disproportionate difference. Although Saddam had loyalists in the party, army and security organs who were neither Tikritis nor his tribesmen, it was his tribesmen, Tikritis, Beijis and Duris, who became the backbone of his security system. Saddam Hussein's brutality has, at times, alienated him from various sections of his own tribe.

An example of this is the house of Abd al-Mun'im, to which Lieutenant General Mahir Abd al-Rashid belongs. The fact that Qusay is married to his daughter Lama did not prevent the president from forcing him to retire, placing him under house arrest at the end of the Iran–Iraq War and then instructing him to avoid Baghdad. Maher's family suspects that Saddam was involved in planning a helicopter accident in which their brother, Brigadier General Tahir, died in the final stages of the Iran–Iraq War.

Where is the Albu-Nasir tribe now?

Members of the Albu-Nasir are to be found in all internal security organisations and military bodies, but the fact that the tribe is no more than 30,000 strong means that their concentrations vary: close to the president, they are ubiquitous, but they are less evident in the outer circles of power. The presidential guard, or Himaya, which consists of a few thousand young men guarding Saddam's palaces and occasionally providing his security escort, is made up almost exclusively of Albu-Nasir men. Most have little formal education, but they are all well trained as bodyguards and know what discipline means. Their commanders, too, hail from the tribe. Himaya loyalty to Saddam is near absolute; and it is difficult to imagine that they would defect as long as he was alive, or as long as they believed he was. They are tough and when necessary cruel. And while they are no match for a Western army in a head-on confrontation, they could prove to be dangerous in house-to-house, hand-to-hand combat where a Western army could not deploy attack helicopters or heavy armour.

The Albu-Nasir are also found in central positions in all the other internal security bodies. Most importantly, they control the Special Security Organisation (*jihaz al-amn al-khass*, SSO), the most feared and important internal security body in Iraq. It is responsible for ensuring the loyalty of all security and military personnel, coordinating the activities of the other bodies protecting the president and the regime's luminaries, and controlling the missiles and other weapons of mass destruction (WMD) launch platforms. Without their total loyalty and support it is doubtful that Saddam could survive for more than a few weeks.

The Albu-Nasir are also very prominent, mainly as officers, in the Special Republican Guard (SRG), which is responsible for the security of Baghdad and the Tikrit area. Saddam ensures the loyalty even of people whose family members he has had executed or assassinated, by promoting them, or retaining them in important positions where they cannot reach him personally. He also surrounds them with informers who report any suspicious actions. In this way, tribe members whom he no longer trusts can still be of value to him.

Other Tikriti tribes and groups

In addition to the Albu-Nasir, there are a few other tribes and groups closely aligned with Saddam and his tribe. They live as neighbours of the Albu-Nasir, mainly in Tikrit itself, the village of al-Uja and the towns of Beiji and Dur. Most of them are loyal to the president and are extremely important for his security and political dominance, but at least some are partially estranged from the regime. The most important of those are the Jawa'ina. This tribe, from the vicinity of the town of Haditha, on the Euphrates northwest of Baghdad, was the most important in the Tikrit area under the monarchy. In the early 1970s, Saddam executed General Hussein Hiyawi, the commander of the Air Force (and a Jawa'ina). In 1993 he executed General Raji Abbas al-Tikriti, ex-commander of the army's medical corps, and Jasim Amin Mukhlis – the famous Mawlud

Mukhlis's nephew – suspecting them of hatching a coup against him. Overall, Saddam has put to death scores of his Tikriti colleagues and yet, Tikriti support for him has not seemed to wane. Here, too, the privileges enjoyed by Tikritis are so great, and the fear of retribution against them so overwhelming that, generally speaking, the people of Saddam's hometown and its environs are still supportive of his regime.

The town of Tikrit and its environs are central to the command of the armed forces. For example, the post of chief of staff has been filled since 2000 by General Ibrahim Abd al-Sattar Muhammad al-Tikriti. In the past, the commanders of the Air Force – an extremely sensitive position, due to the risk that a plane could attack the Presidential Palace rather than the enemy – were Generals Hamid Sha'ban, and Muzahim Sa'b Hasan, both Tikritis and members of Saddam's tribe. Today, it is commanded by General Hamid Raja Shallah, not a tribe member but still a Tikriti. In the period 1991–2002, two or three of the five army group commanders were always Tikritis. At present, the two Tikritis are Sulayman Yusif Twayni, commander of the First Army Group in the north, and General Ra'd Abd al-Majid Faysal, commander of the Third Army Group in the south.

Likewise, most of the divisional commanders in the Republican Guard are Tikritis. Given the size of the town, the representation of Tikriti officers at the top of the command system is astonishing. Choosing the high command of the army and Republic Guard from such a small segment of a population of 23 million may be a dubious guarantee of quality and creates much resentment in the army – hardly conducive to high morale – but it does guarantee political control.

Regional affinities have always been strong in Iraq, and occasionally tribal affinities as well. Such affinities are conducive to political loyalty, but must be enhanced by additional components, such as socio-economic privileges and political power. Saddam Hussein has proven himself to be a master manipulator of this kind of patronage. Yet, even he could not prevent clashes with some military commanders from his own tribe and region. Tribal-regional affinity and perks are not enough to guarantee total loyalty. Some became disillusioned about the direction in which Saddam was leading the nation after he attacked Iran. Since the end of the Iran–

Iraq War there has been one attempted *coup d'état* by the J\
in 1990. This resulted in arrests and executions. Many Ju\
officers whose participation was uncertain were pensioned o\
the early 1990s some prominent Ubaydis were singled out by
regime as would-be revolutionaries, but today, loyal Jubburis and
Ubaydis are still fairly prominent in the regime. Thus, for example,
the Minister for Oil, who is also very central in Iraq's weapons
industry, is Amir Rashid al-Ubaydi. Still, Saddam has managed to
instil in them sufficient fear to stem further *coups d'état* against him.
Others despise him for his pretension to military omniscience
despite having never served in the armed forces, or for his brutality.

The outer circles: friendly tribes

Although practically all tribes in the Sunni Arab areas were accorded
benefits, some were more privileged than others by virtue of their
closeness to Saddam Hussein and his tribe. These tribes included,
until a few years ago, tribes neighbouring the Tikrit area (mostly
residing in the Salah al-Din governorate): the Jubbur in Sharqat; the
Ubayd in al-Alam and Tarmiya; the Mushahada in Tarmiya; the
Luhayb in Sharqat; and al-Azza in Balad. A little further a field are
the Harb in Dur; the Tayy in Mosul (the Minister of Defence, General
Sultan Hashim hails from this tribe); the Khazraj from around
Mosul; and the Maghamis from Khalis. However, the largest Sunni-
Arab tribal federations of the Dulaim west of Baghdad and the
Shammar Jarba northwest of Baghdad in Jazira, too, collaborated
with the regime, although less enthusiastically.

Tikritis in the internal security apparatuses

After the party came to power in 1968, by appointing his own people
and purging party old-timers Saddam gradually turned the party
internal security arm, Jihaz Hinin (the Apparatus of Yearning) –
which eventually became the Mukhabarat, or General Intelligence
(GI) – into a docile body totally dedicated to him personally, rather
than to the party, to Ba'athist ideology or to the president. Like Stalin
in the 1920s, Saddam needed about a decade to oust his elderly
relative from power, Ahmad Hasan al-Bakr, founder of Ba'ath rule in
Iraq. Saddam dismantled the old guard, though less rigorously,
within the state General Security Organisation, and created a
number of new bodies from the bottom up. As usual, he secured

the loyalty of his men with a combination of fear and rewards. Middle- and high-level internal security officers are under even greater threat than ordinary Iraqis if they should betray the president or err in their duty. At the same time, they are rewarded more handsomely than most. While it is their job to spy on every Iraqi citizen, including senior army officers, their own colleagues watch them just as diligently. An oversight – or worse, neglecting one's duty – can draw severe punishment, even death. Thus, while security officers have practically unlimited powers over the citizens of Iraq, they themselves are under constant threat. Almost all the internal security organs contain a special unit who watch over their own organisation and root out dissent. The SSO and, to a lesser extent, some other organisations also have the responsibility of monitoring other organisations and the armed forces.

As noted above, the single most important security body is the SSO. One of the newest security bodies, it was established by Hussein Kamil in the mid-1980s. Originally, it numbered around 500 men. In 2002 its strength is unknown, but it may be assumed that with more duties came more staff, and the force must now be at least three times larger. Many of its members hold officer's rank, with the most junior SSO officer effectively outranking the most senior regular army officer. He would be able to plunge those around him into a state of terror. The SSO is mainly in charge of managing the operations of the Special Republican Guard through a special office within the SRG, and of securing the loyalty of its officers, as well as those of the armed forces.[1] The SSO also monitors the other internal security bodies, including the General Intelligence (Mukhabarat) leadership.

The SSO is the ultimate body responsible for the protection of the president. It is also in charge of the concealment of the non-conventional weapons and all the relevant scientific documentation, with an emphasis on non-conventional missile warheads. In concealment and deception they are helped by select officers from the SRG and RG. The SSO also supervises the firing of these missiles once they have been deployed. The most sensitive duties regarding WMD are entrusted to officers who are Saddam's closest blood relations.[2] (This is probably the internal security body that contains the highest percentage of educated and highly intelligent men). Their loyalty is believed to be unshakeable. Given the centrality of the SSO to regime survival, it is not surprising that the two people in command are Qusay Saddam Hussein and his chief aide, the highly experienced General Abd Hamid (or Ihmid) Mahmud (or Hmud)[3].

The Himaya's main responsibility is to guard the president and the regime's luminaries. The Himaya is commanded by a small group of 2–5 men, the companions or *murafiqin*. The organisation is split into two units, 'Special Place' (al-Maqam al-Khass) under Rukan Abd al-Ghafur Sulayman Razuqi (the brother of the Himaya commander), who is also in charge of the president's tribal contacts. This unit is in charge of protecting the palaces and Saddam's other homes. The other detachment is called 'the Weapons' (*al-silah*). They are in charge of protecting the president when he travels around Iraq. Until 2000, they were commanded by Arshad Yasin, and then, until mid-2002, by Muzahim Sa'b Hasan, both members of Saddam's tribe. General Intelligence (the Mukhabarat-GI), focuses on anti-opposition activities at home as well as information gathering and terrorist activities abroad.[4] Tikritis numbers at the high and middle levels of GI are also high, even greater than in the other security-related organisations – General Security, the Republican Guard and the Special Republican Guard.

Yet another large organisation with offices and prisons all over Iraq is General Security (al-Amn al-Amm – GS), which reports to the Minister of the Interior. Its chief is, or was until recently, Tikriti Major General Tahir Jalil Habush. There are other, less important but still fairly effective internal security bodies, such as Military Intelligence that, in addition to the classical duties of similar bodies elsewhere, is involved in counter-espionage, and monitoring, arresting and torturing civilians. The chief of Military Intelligence is, or was until 2000, Major General Mu'tamad Ni'ma al-Tikriti, a member of the Beijat, Saddam's sub-tribal unit, and a former commander of the al-Nida Division in the RG. There may be no doubt that both chiefs are very close and very loyal to Saddam. (In the writer's judgement, they may be dissuaded from performing atrocities in his service if suitably warned by the US and if the regime looked like it is going to fall). Unfortunately, however, neither the MI nor GS will be important in a fully fledged war.

The Republican Guard is a 60–70,000 strong force armed with some 800 tanks as well as artillery and attack helicopters. Deployed around Baghdad, the Republican Guard is not usually allowed into the city. Its role is to protect Baghdad against an external enemy, but also against the regular army if required.[5] The regular army forms the next ring around the president, but there are always Republican Guard units between it and Baghdad. In the case of an American assault on Iraq, the more loyal units of the Republican Guard may be ordered into the capital to combat the invading army. While the Republican Guard has never trained for such warfare, it can be expected to put up a strong fight all the same, hiding amid Baghdad's civilians. Most or all the divisional commanders of the Republican Guard, and all the brigade commanders of the Special Republican Guard have traditionally been Tikritis.

The SRG is a crucial link in the protection of the regime, and it will be of tremendous value if some of its officers can be persuaded not to support Saddam. The SRG are a well-trained commando force of 20–25,000 men. The SRG is in charge of the protection of Baghdad, Tikrit and a few other places against any attacking force. They are trained to fight in built-up areas against infantry and tanks alike, and they have ground-to-air defences, around 100 tanks, artillery and a large number of anti-tank weapons. They can substantially delay the advance of any force that tries to enter the capital city. They will not hesitate to use Baghdad's civilians as live shields, and their loyalty to Saddam is, so far, solid. I believe that until it is clear to them that all is lost, they will fight. Another duty of the SRG is, in the event of a Shi'ite revolt against Saddam, to surround and bombard the two main Shi'ite quarters of Baghdad: the two million-strong slum Madinat Saddam, east of the city centre; and the ancient quarter of Kazimayn, where there is a magnificent mosque and where two of the 12 Shi'ite *imams* are buried. If there is a revolt against the regime in one of these quarters, and Madinat Saddam is a very likely candidate, there must be a way of dissuading the SRG from opening fire, otherwise the casualties will be horrendous. A high-profile threat that war crimes would be punished after the conflict by trial and capital punishment may work once the regime's survival is in doubt.

Other security organisations include Uday Saddam Hussein's Fida'iyyin and the border police. The least politicised security organisation is the police force, which, like General Security, operates under the responsibility of the Minister of the Interior.

The loyalty of the officer corps is continually tested by the regime. Failure to report sedition can bring severe punishment. One technique may be called the Trojan horse: an officer will express critical views of Saddam in a discussion with a colleague. The colleague faces a dilemma: if he does not report the incident to the SSO or Military Security (al-Amn al-Askari – MS) and the officer is an *agent provocateur*, then he will be imprisoned or at least demoted and expelled from the army. However, if the discussion was genuine, he will be landing his colleague in severe trouble. (Such talk can also get the dissenter's tongue cut out).[6] This system is no secret. It is in the regime's interest to promote widespread public awareness of it. Individuals will thus rush to report to the authorities any case of incitement. In this way, the public police themselves. Unlike most other internal security bodies, even the Himaya, most officers in the SSO will not forsake Saddam even when they believe that he is on his way down. Their fate is so intimately tied with his by now that they will support him to the end. Furthermore, they are the only ones (perhaps with a few SRG officers) who know where the most lethal WMD are hidden. Even after Saddam is gone, they are likely to use them, either as bargaining chips or in their own defence.

Tikritis in the Republican Guard and Special Republican Guard

There is no reliable and comprehensive information on the percentage of Tikritis in the Republican Guard, or among its officers. In addition to the fact that the Secretary General of the Republican Guard is Saddam Hussein's distant paternal cousin, no less than 50% of the divisional commanders have always been Tikritis, Nasiris or Duris. The commander of the Republican Guard, by contrast, has often been a non-Tikriti, as is the case in 2002, but he has always been a staunch loyalist. Probably the most interesting example is General Iyad Khalifa al-Rawi, who commanded the invasion of Kuwait and who in 2002 is the commander of a new military unit Saddam is building, the Jerusalem Army. He is a party old-timer and a good field commander whose personal loyalty to Saddam has been proverbial. This does not mean that Republican Guard officers, including Tikritis, have never plotted against the regime. As noted above, in summer 1996, a number of them were executed for such a plot, and from time to time there are reports of executions. Nevertheless, the

Republican Guard has proved generally loyal to president and regime.

According to a reasonably well-informed ex-colonel in the Iraqi armed forces, Ahmad al-Zaidi,[7] by the end of the 1990s just over 80% of its officers hailed from the governorate of Salah al-Din, where Tikrit, Ujah, Dur and Beiji are situated. Zaidi believes that most of them are from Tikrit.[8] According to the colonel, officers from Mosul represent about 10% of the SRG, officers from Anbar some 9% and officers from Baghdad around 5%. Even if Zaidi's information is exaggerated, there is no reason to doubt the fact that more than 50% of the officers holding the most significant jobs in the SRG are either Tikritis or come from Salah al-Din.

Governors of provinces

Since the Gulf War, the regime's tendency has been to nominate ex-military men as governors, in contrast to the earlier practice in which civilian senior party officials were preferred. Often these governors appear in military uniform with their military rank mentioned in media coverage. Between 1998 and 2002, a few, though not the majority, of the governors were Tikritis. Thus, for example, Lieutenant General Muhammad Fayzi al-Haza, a member of Saddam's tribe, was governor of Maysan (Amara) until at least 2000, possibly until 2002.[9] The governor of Baghdad province, including the capital, is Lieutenant General Sabir al-Duri.[10] The governor of Basra from 1998 until at least 2000 was Lieutenant General Ahmad Ibrahim Hamash al-Tikriti (an ex-RG officer).[11] The governor of Salah-al-Din province is a party civilian, Ahmad Abd Rashid, a member of Saddam's tribe.[12]

The number of troops available to provincial governors is limited, but it is sufficient to put down local revolts, and this is their main task. Any one who wishes to encourage the local population, especially in the south, to rise against the regime must find a way to discourage these governors from crushing such a revolt, a question that invasion planners should be thinking about. One approach would be to promise that such action would be subject to prosecution after the war. As long as the regime is stable, or the governor is under that impression, such a threat will not carry any weight. However, the moment there is a sense that the regime is about to fall, people may well respond to such a warning.

The ruling party

Unlike the armed forces and the internal security apparatuses, the party has always been less clearly controlled by Tikritis and other people hailing from the Salah al-Din governorate, although they are still prominent. Just before and after the Gulf War, around 28–29% of the members of the Iraqi Regional Leadership (RL) of the party were Tikritis. If one adds the Duris, whose number in the RL increased at the September 1991 regional congress from one to three, by the end of 1991 Tikritis and Duris together formed 47% of the Iraqi Regional Leadership. Following the Eleventh Regional Congress of July 1995, out of 18 members there were five Tikritis (28%) and one Duri (5.5%), a total of 33.5%. Despite the decrease, the number of people from Salah al-Din was still very high. It is important to point out that the increased representation of Tikritis and Duris came at the expense of the Shia party activists. Thus, in early 1991, 36% of the RL were Shias, whereas by later that same year, the percentage had dropped to 12%. At the time of writing, Shi'ite representation rose slightly (4–5 out 19).

Further down the party hierarchy (secretaries of bureaus, branches and smaller branches *maktab, far', shu'ba*) Tikritis and Duris are still prominent, but the lower one goes the fewer one finds. Nevertheless, as in other domains already discussed, their representation by far exceeds the representation of Tikrit within the Iraqi population as a whole. In the lower echelons, the number and percentage of Shia party activists increases significantly, whereas Tikritis and other Sunni-Arab activists are relatively few. By allowing Shia members to dominate the lower and middle levels of the party, where contact with the public is most extensive, it seems that the regime hopes to give the Shia majority a sense of participation and presence in running the party, while at the same time ensuring that the key positions at upper levels are dominated by Tikritis, Duris and other Sunnis.

The party branches control the party militia in the various provinces. As long as the regime seems stable, there is no reason to expect any upheavals. Following the 1991 Shia uprising, local party organisations have taken measures to stop any future uprisings. However, in the face of a military offensive that seems likely to topple the regime, party activists can hardly be expected to save the regime, let alone fight to the death for it. In the Shia areas, Tikriti and other Sunni-Arab party officials will leave, possibly with their Shia comrades. In the Sunni-Arab areas, they will stay, but they do not have much to fight with. Following the demise of the regime, some of them may well go into hiding, or even try to establish underground cells, with the help of Tikriti intelligence and internal security officers.

Tikriti vulnerability

The two people who control the Himaya, or Presidential Protection, are Saddam's younger son, Qusay, and Lieutenant General Abd al-Hamid Mahmud, helped by the small group of *murafiqin*, all members of Saddam's tribe. This author has no idea how to dissuade these people from supporting Saddam. He is fully dependent on them, but they too are fully dependent on him. Nor do I believe there is a way of dissuading the SSO – which Qusay and Mahmud also control – from supporting Saddam to the end. Both organisations have carried out so many bloody missions for Saddam that if Saddam fell they would be under great threat from many families in Iraq, Sunni as well as Shia, and even Tikriti.

During a period of fighting, it is unlikely that the Tikritis can be dissuaded from supporting Saddam; however, there are two approaches that should be tried. First, all officers must be warned, time and again, that any order on their part to use WMD will have dire consequences for them personally. The officers of the SSO are very dedicated to president and regime. The SSO personnel are bright and extremely confident, and this may provide some hope that if the right arguments reach them they may be persuaded not to push the buttons. Most of them hail from the province of Salah al-Din, mainly from Tikrit, Beiji and Dur. Many of them have moved into Baghdad with their families. It is not difficult to identify those areas in Baghdad where they and their families live, together with the families of many regime luminaries: the most senior party echelon, the more senior officers of the RG and SRG and even the most senior army generals. If one wants to influence the SSO and, to an extent, the SRG and RG officers, the best way is to persuade them that Saddam Hussein is ready to sacrifice Baghdad if the city is about to fall into the hands of his opponents. One way of doing this is to make it known to them that retaliation for a non-conventional attack against American-British troops, Kuwait, Turkey, the Kurdish region or Israel will be overwhelming. Whether or not this is indeed what the coalition forces intend to do is irrelevant: the important task is to convince those officers that such a non-conventional attack will mean the total destruction of the Salah al-Din governorate and Baghdad.

Alternatively, it could be relayed to them that, rather than Baghdad as a whole, those areas where the political and security elite reside will be completely obliterated by precision strikes. These specific areas may in fact be mentioned when a message is sent to the Tikriti officers of the SSO, SRG and RG. It will be important to convince them, or, at least to point out to them, that in 1991 Saddam's orders were designed to bring about a nuclear Israeli attack against Baghdad if he thought Baghdad was about to fall to the Allied forces. His *modus operandi* during the Gulf War was, quite clearly, that if he could not retain control of Baghdad, then he would prefer to see its five million inhabitants perish. If the RG, SRG and SSO officers understand that, there is a hope that, once it is clear that Baghdad is about to fall, they will turn against their own leader to prevent total destruction.

It should be stated very clearly that this author has no knowledge at all what the true American and Israeli plans are for such an eventuality, but Saddam's Tikriti officers have to be made aware that such a possibility exists.

The second approach to dissuade officers from fighting would be a public and high profile promise by the US and British governments, and the Iraqi opposition, that if no further war crimes occur, only a very limited number of people will be prosecuted. The names of those to be prosecuted will be published beforehand, namely: Saddam Hussein, his two sons, Abd al-Hamid Mahmud, Izzat Ibrahim, Taha Yasin Ramadan and no more than ten or 20 other key regime members. Officers and soldiers of the Himaya, SSO and SRG should be promised that, if they defect, they will be well treated and not persecuted in any way. However, if they fight until the end it must be made clear that they will be arrested as prisoners of war, put on trial and that they may languish in prison for a long time. If their property came to them from Saddam, it will be returned to the nation.

Once the regime is toppled, those numerous Tikritis who bear grudges against the regime should be approached to become the

representatives of the Tikritis, Duris and others from this area in
their contacts with the new regime. They could also play a useful
role in assuring their relatives and neighbours that their legitimate
interests are being respected.

An additional approach that may be adopted, as part of
psychological warfare, is to broadcast to the various military and
security units at a crucial moment that Saddam is dead and buried
under the rubble of one of his shelters. This must be done when no
broadcasts of the regime can be heard. During the fighting, most
officers will have no way of telling where Saddam is, and when they
realise that Baghdad TV and radio are mute, or better still, that they
have been taken over by coalition forces, there is a good chance they
will stop fighting.

The Tikritis after the war

The greatest danger at the last stage of the war and immediately
following the cessation of hostilities is that the SSO and some
Himaya or SRG units will retain weapons of mass destruction. The
SSO are by far the most likely to control these weapons, and are also
among those with most to lose as a result of regime change. They
will be desperate and extremely dangerous. A negotiating team must
be ready to step in immediately in the event they are trapped and
give them assurances for their safety. A massive effort must be made
to locate those weapons even before such a situation is created.
Likewise, captured SSO officers must be persuaded to provide
information on the whereabouts of these weapons and their comrades
in arms. These people will conceivably have the means to kill many
thousands of their own citizens, as well as many coalition soldiers,
with the push of a button even after the fighting is over. Their capture
and interrogation must be the coalition's highest priority.

In the wake of hostilities, Himaya, SSO and SRG soldiers and
officers will have to be pensioned off. No new regime can count on
their loyalty, ever. Yet such a massive release from military service is
fraught with dangers. These are people who know each other, have
combat skills, understand discipline, have experienced commanders
and share the same provenance. Last but not least, they will have
hidden weapons and ammunition caches. If not stopped right away,
they will almost certainly become either a political underground
organisation that will topple the regime the moment the foreign

armies leave, or a formidable mafia organisation, or both. Even before the foreign armies leave, they could become an underground or criminal organisation that could assassinate US and British soldiers and officers in Iraq. The US has a track record of withdrawing the moment a terrorist group draws American blood: Beirut and Mogadishu are examples every Iraqi has been reminded of frequently. Iraqis also know what happened in Afghanistan, but US stamina there has not yet been tested to the full. The prudent course therefore would be to quarantine the aforementioned units for 1–6 months. The first to be released will be those who gave themselves up; indeed, these men should receive better prison conditions than those who fought to the end. Those who are pensioned off should be considered 'on parole', with reporting and monitoring required by probationary procedures. They must be encouraged to re-integrate themselves into the economic system. After years of having high salaries, cars and homes, and enjoying high social status, this will be very difficult for them. A special authority should be established to assist this process of demobilisation. The Tikritis will be high on the list of those needing such assistance. Returning middle- and low-level civilian party officials to productive life will be easier, but it will not be easy. The Tikritis among them will have to be withdrawn from many positions throughout Iraq and returned to their own area.

Iraq will still need an army, and senior officers, including Tikritis, who performed no atrocities should be allowed to continue their military service. But the Republican Guard should be dissolved: Iraq does not need two armies. RG officers without a criminal record should be transferred to the army, but as individuals, not *en masse*. As for politicians, those of them who will not be brought to trial will have to be released into the custody of their wives but they, too, will have to report to their local police station. These people know how to run an underground movement and should be monitored for at least a few months.

As for the Tikrit area (Salah al-Din Governorate) and the parts of Baghdad inhabited by the present elite, all exits from these compounds are currently being monitored by the Iraqi government. This monitoring should continue after the regime is toppled, to prevent a *coup d'état*. Keeping the former elite in this virtual prison also serves the purpose of preventing an onslaught of looting and vengeance by Baghdad's (mostly Shia) poor. In this way the weeks during which the previous elite will be in *de facto* quarantined can be seen by them as a protective as well as a preventive measure, preventing the poor masses from massacring them and, at the same time, stopping the ex-elite reforming to destabilise the new political order.

Conclusion

The combination of large and powerful bodyguard units and internal security and intelligence organs has protected Saddam Hussein and his regime. It can be expected to work reasonably well until a regime collapse is believed to be inevitable. Then, the ones who may be expected to remain loyal to the president are the SSO, the Himaya, most of the SRG and probably the heavy divisions of the Republican Guard. The regular army will not be ready to die for Saddam, and the various intelligence organs will be largely irrelevant in the case of a major war. However, short of a major American assault on Iraq, the system may be expected to hold.

As pointed out above, fear is not a sufficient incentive to generate long-term loyalty. Saddam has also provided his supporters with socio-economic benefits. Since 1999, he has managed to amass around $2 billion annually from economic activity outside of the UN sponsored oil-for-food programme, which, in addition to his savings from the fat years, provides him with sufficient resources to pamper his supporters. Out of 23 million Iraqis, he only need buy off no more than one million people. Well-organised and well-equipped, this one million controls the whole of Iraq.

The regular army protects the regime's borders against infiltration by guerrilla activities (mainly around the southern marshes and the Iran–Iraq border) and foreign armies. The RG and a number of internal security apparatuses protect the president against the regular army. The internal security bodies (mainly the SSO, a section within military intelligence and the party's Military Bureau) monitor the behaviour of the officer corps. All these bodies also monitor the RG. The SRG protects the capital city against the RG and the regular army. And the Himaya, with the SRG, protects the president against any attempted *coup d'état* in Baghdad or Tikrit.

The internal security bodies overlap: at least two or three of them monitor the same bodies and almost all of them monitor the population at large. Most of them have their own prisons and interrogation centres, and an army officer or any citizen may become a victim to any one or several of them. There is no doubt that the system is far from being cost effective. However, because internal security is such a high priority, the regime considers the extra cost a good investment. In the final analysis, the system is quite effective. Having said this, the Tikritis are not a unified or even a homogenous group. While many of them enjoy special privileges under the present regime, others have suffered greatly under Saddam Hussein. Some, without a doubt, are loyal to him personally and will risk their lives in his defence, but many others, probably the vast majority of them, support him out of sheer expediency, and his disappearance and the change of circumstances will very likely change their loyalties. Others have tried to topple him despite the benefits of his patronage. They are dead, but they have relatives and friends who cannot forget what Saddam has done. Some will be outraged at the change of regime and will try to use their military experience and skills to keep ahead of the pack in a post-Saddam Iraq, or even to bring back Tikriti dominance. However, most will probably prefer to seek integration into the new social and political order. The main task of any occupying force during the first months of occupation will be to differentiate between these two groups: to keep under surveillance, or even imprison, those dangerous to the new regime; but also to open the door to those who are ready and willing to live in a post-Saddam, post-Tikriti Iraq, based on the principle of meritocracy, rather than tribal and regional affiliation.

There are a few areas where Tikriti and non-Tikriti Ba'athis alike should not be allowed any influence or involvement for years after Saddam is toppled: finance, education, the military and internal security, and the media. Senior- and middle-level Ba'athists who rose through the ranks have become themselves living examples of the party's supercilious, chauvinistic and simplistic nature. In a post-Saddam Iraq in which they have lost their social, economic and political privileges, they will do everything in their power to 'Ba'athise' Iraq again, to recover their lost paradise. Many of them truly believe in some of the party's ideals. While the concepts of socialism and secularism are now dead, the concepts of Arab-Islamic power – military might and political control by a selected elite – are very much alive. Furthermore, the concept that Saddam introduced, beginning in the 1970s, of Iraqi dominance over an Arab empire, is still very much alive, as reflected by the Iraqi media. The only change, which occurred mainly in the 1990s, is that now the aspiration for Iraqi dominance, imperial rule or hegemony is occasionally extended to the Muslim world as a whole. Ba'athists feel the deepest disdain for truly democratic values and a strong hatred for the West. Such people must be prevented from having any positions of influence. On the other hand, Ba'athist officials can play an important role in technical areas where professional expertise is badly needed: communication, irrigation (provided they do not use their positions to gain support from tribes), electricity, in municipal services and so on. Iraq will need every skilled person, and totally excluding Ba'athists will deprive the new Iraq of essential human resources.

Notes

1 See for example Ali Abd al-Amir reporting from Amman, *al-Hayat*, July 13, 2001, on the execution by the SSO of two air force pilots near Kirkuk in front of officers of the air base of al-Huriyya.

2 As reported to this author by a senior UNSCOM inspector.

3 Based on interviews with four senior UNSCOM officials in the US in 1996-99 and 2002, and with 'Umar', an Iraqi engineer who renovated one of Saddam's palaces and knew some of the second generation of the ruling elite. He left the country in 1990 (Washington, D.C. January 1994); and see: Scott Ritter, *Endgame Solving the Iraq Problem – Once and For All* (New York, Simon and Schuster, 1999), pp. 18, 77, 85-87, 90-92, 97, 102, 107-108, 112, 124-26, 141-43, 151, 163-75, 187; Amatzia Baram, 'The Iraqi Armed Forces and Security Apparatus', in *Journal of Conflict, Security and Development* (King's College, Univ. of London), 1:2 (2001), 113-23; *Jane's Sentinel Security Assessment*, The Gulf States, May-Oct. 2000 (internet version: www.Janes.com).

4 Regis Matlak, *Inside Saddam's Grip: An Open Source Memorandum*, a draft article, Washington DC, January 23, 1999, p. 15.

5 An interview with a senior UNSCOM head of team who had to study the SSO and the SRG as part of his search for Iraqi WMD, 1997.

6 See for example Regis Matlak, *Inside Saddam's Grip*, p. 13. This technique is also described in interviews with Iraqi expatriates and Western intelligence officers.

7 Colonel Ahmad al-Zaidi, *al-Azmina al-Da'i'a: Sha'b Yamut wa Jaysh Yahtadiru* (Damascus, Dar al-Mada lil-Thaqafa wal-Nashr, 2000), pp. 283-317.

8 Other senior officers from the Tikrit area were, for example, brigadier generals and full colonels Najam Abd Allah Hamza al-Duri; Ali Kijwan al-Tikriti; Husayn Ahmad al-Nasiri; Muhammad Taha Hasan Yahya Hunu al-Tikriti; Tha'ir Jalal al-Tikriti; Ghasan Mikhlif al-Tikriti; Barazan Arzij Sulayman al-Majid al-Tikriti (a cousin of Saddam's); Ra'd Daham al-Tikriti; Mu'yyid Najah al-Tikriti; Samy Wahib al-Nasiri; Muhammad Ali Husayn al-Tikriti and others. They are brigade commanders, deputy brigade commanders in charge of the missiles, internal security officers breathing down the necks of those in charge of logistics, training and so on.

9 *Al-Qadisiyya* , April 28, 1998.

10 *Alif Ba*, May 23, 2001.

11 *Al-Thawra*, April 9, 1998.

12 *Al-Jumhuriyya*, August 14, 2001.

Chapter 6

The Iraqi Army and Anti-Army: Some Reflections on the Role of the Military

Faleh A. Jabar

Success or failure for the Ba'ath regime will inevitably be determined by the performance and cohesion of the Iraqi army. The army's cohesion is conditional on a set of complex factors, often neglected, crucially the unity of the ruling elite or clan–class and the nature of the coming conflict. The conventional wisdom is that as soon as the coalition campaign is unleashed the regular army will readily lay down its arms, while the more coherent Republican Guard may put up a fierce fight. According to this understanding of the situation, the Republican Guard is better motivated, better equipped and better paid than the regular units, hence more loyal and more willing to fight. By contrast, the regular units are dispirited, poorly equipped and poorly paid.[1]

This juxtaposition of elite forces with the regular army is oversimplified and perhaps misleading. It reduces the causes of cohesion or disintegration to important, but loosely generalised, military factors and ignores the complex nature of war and politics, the interaction of the political system, the ruling class, their sway over the military machine, and the nature of the pending war itself. This paper will examine potential trends in the armed forces within the wider context of Iraqi politics. This examination relies heavily on past experiences (the 1958 coup, the 1980–88 Iran–Iraq War, the 1990–91 Gulf War and the uprisings in its aftermath) and is speculative or hypothetical in character.

The armed forces under the Ba'ath: major structural changes

The Ba'ath regime returned to power for the second time in 1968. Its leaders were traumatised by the experience of the preceding decade of military rule: the incessant threat of a military takeover and the menace of a disunited officer corps. Varied sources of ruling elite cohesion had been experimented with under previous regimes: military discipline under General Qassim (1958–63), ideological unity under the first Ba'athist regime (February–November 1963) and a combination of tribal solidarity and military discipline under the Arif brothers' rule (1963–68). The Eighth Ba'ath Party Congress of 1974 set the Party two goals. Firstly, to subsume the army under the party's control, purging its ranks of 'suspicious, conspiratorial and adventurous elements' and to indoctrinate its members fully. In a word, to 'Ba'athise' the army, or in the official jargon to create an 'indoctrinated army'. Secondly, it wanted to restructure, modernise and expand the army.[2]

As regime security was the ultimate goal, the Ba'athisation of the army was a necessary, but not sufficient way of controlling the military. By injecting kinship and clan groupings into every level of the army, the regime added a much stronger guarantee of loyalty. The end result was a two-tier system: the party controlled the military and the clan controlled the party. The party grew from a few hundred members and few thousand followers in 1968 to an organisation of 1,800,000 [in 1979], of which at least 10% were full-fledged members.[3] The party provided the mass manpower needed for surveillance and control, while the clan delivered bonds of trust. By dint of modern norms and traditional values, both produced discipline and obedience. The clan and kinship networks delivered trusted individuals to key positions within the party and wider governing structures. The tribal alliance that grew to control state-party institutions became stratified, with different clans assuming different roles within the hierarchy. The Bejat clan assumed a role that can be understood as 'royal', while the Doori, Rawi, Dulaimi, Juboori and others assumed lower positions equivalent to 'Earls', 'Lords' and 'Sirs' respectively.

In addition to injecting the party and army with networks of clan and kinship, the coercive tools of state control were radically reorganised. Intricate and overlapping chains of command and control were created. The leadership of the party's Military Bureau were given responsibility for the selection of cadets and organising men in uniform. The National Security Council controlled all the intelligence and security organs. The Ministry of Defence, the Air Force and the Republican Guard all became dominated by those associated with the leadership by clan and kinship. In addition to the General Chief of Staff, three other centres of control were created: the party's military bureau; the National Security Bureau (in charge of intelligence and security); and the informal kinship networks.

This overlapping structure has given the president a freer hand in supervision, control and management. While this arrangement personalises command and control mechanisms, it enables the president to bypass the vertical chain of command and reach out directly to control any area of the military. During the Iran–Iraq War, complaints about this form of control came from within the military. While this personalisation of control mechanisms has served the domestic regime security well, it is a distinct handicap to operational capability in modern warfare.

The army was also given a dual structure, split between the regular army and the Republican Guard. After the removal of the Arif regime in 1968, the Republican Guard was developed into a fully-fledged corps, then further expanded to an army of two corps. This double organisation seems to imply a conscious differentiation between regime security and national defence, although the Republican Guard took an active part both in the first and second Gulf wars.

During this process of military reconstruction, the social origins of the senior military commanders and the role of the armed forces changed radically. This has brought about the gradual decline of the officer corps' political role and the return of the army to the barracks after more than a decade of political intervention.

Military personnel formed 100% of the first Revolutionary Command Council (RCC), Iraq's supreme ruling body. Of the 15 members of the second RCC formed in 1971, only five were officers (33%). This percentage kept decreasing until, in 1979 when Saddam Hussein took over, there were no military members of the RCC. A new generation of commanders, who were totally submissive and answerable to the politicians, had been gradually imposed on the military. In the words of the historian Majid Khadduri, 'the Ba'ath was the first regime to bring the army under civilian control'.[4]

In addition to these qualitative changes, there has been a quantitative leap in the size of the military establishment, with a large expansion in manpower, armament and logistics. As the end of the era of soldier-politician began, a new era of the colossal army began. In just over a decade, the armed forces grew from approximately 50,000 in 1968 to 430,000 in 1980, a 10-fold increase. The army's ratio to population rose from roughly 6 per 1,000 to more than 31 per 1,000. This rapid growth reflected both the regime's stability as well as its grand regional designs.

The devouring Leviathan: the legacy of the two Gulf Wars

The Iraq–Iran war ushered the nation, the military included, into a period of turmoil, uncertainty and change. Oil wealth, world and regional support, and the union of popular patriotism and official nationalism, sustained the Iraqi war effort. Yet, the army that emerged from the war differed from that which entered it. First, the armed forces grew to roughly one million men-under-arms. This did not include the paramilitary organisations of the party militia (the Popular Army), or the 150,000 or so men who made up the Kurdish tribal mercenary units, dubbed the Battalions of National Defence. War depleted Iraq's resources and plunged it into huge debt, estimated at between $40–50 billion. As Iraq emerged from the war a mighty military power, it was economically crippled. War fatigue, economic hardships and social dislocation caused by the regime's policies brought the war generation to the brink of rebellion. Party and kinship networks, once highly dense, grew thin. To the leadership the army posed the threat of turning into an uncontrollable Leviathan.

During the 1988–90 inter-war period, cracks in the union of popular and official nationalisms began to surface among the restless war generation. The biggest dilemma was how to feed the one million men in uniform and how to finance their dignified return to civilian life. Hailed as Saddam's heroes and the nation's brave men, they were feared by the ruling elite for their restive behaviour. Two potential outcomes came to dominate the regime's considerations. In one, angry and hungry demobilised soldiers plagued civilian life, causing an upsurge in disorder and criminality. The second possible outcome envisaged an implosion of the army if they were kept under arms for any length of time. Extra economic resources were desperately needed to pacify the army. Political reforms to ease tensions were also discussed. The invasion of Kuwait, a remedy of sorts, spectacularly backfired. The humiliating defeat and heavy human losses turned the misadventure into a catalyst for disintegration and mutiny. The 1991 uprising, in which sections of the military were key players, marked the disintegration of the army.

The sundry roles soldiers played at the end of the 1991 Gulf War revealed three major but contradictory trends: mutiny; capitulation; and cohesion. These trends already existed before the outbreak of hostilities. Desertion was a problem before 1990, and the potential for mutiny was even higher. After the start of the land war, soldiers voted with their feet. Most units in the Kuwaiti theatre did not put up much of a fight, with more than 70,000 surrendering during the first day of fighting.

However, mutiny, capitulation and cohesion, came fully to the fore in the wake of the ceasefire. Mutiny and desertion leading to total disintegration characterised operations in the southern theatre. In the north, military units, totalling some 150,000 soldiers, laid down their arms, determined neither to rebel nor to defend the regime. However, in the middle sector centring on Baghdad, a much greater degree of cohesion and loyalty was maintained and effectively deployed by the regime.

How can the mutinies that overwhelmed the south and the north, and the sharp contrast with steadfast allegiance of the middle sector, be explained? Firstly, there was a strong and generalised sense of apathy toward the 'Kuwait War', as the soldiers dubbed it. A great deal of war fatigue was left over from the Iraq–Iran war, which destroyed the old union between official and popular nationalisms, and drove them into opposition. Heavy casualties, poor logistics, meagre provisions, operational mismanagement, defeat and a disorganised withdrawal augmented a sense of bitterness in the units stationed in the south. In addition, party commissars and loyal kinship networks were sparsely represented in the units sent to the south and those left in Kuwait.

Paradoxically, the devastating coalition air campaign, which initially triggered an over-radicalised reaction on the part of the withdrawing soldiers in the south, ultimately wiped out the bulk of these angry and retreating forces. A quantitative approach to regional power relations (Iraq versus Iran) overshadowed US calculations, which unwittingly overlooked a possible qualitative appreciation of the domestic role these units could have played in the removal of the regime. The other irony is that the air campaign helped rid Saddam Hussein of the menace posed by the routed army in the southern sector. Soon after withdrawal, the scattered and disorganised units revolted. One retreating tank, upon reaching Basra, aimed and fired at a colossal wall poster of Saddam Hussein in the city centre. That was the first spark of the uprisings. However, in a matter of days, the various rebellious groups had dissolved.

In the north, there were some common and divergent factors at work, prominent among which were the mutinies staged by both the *Mustasharin*, commanders of the Kurdish tribal battalions, and the mobilised urban population. Sensing defeat and isolation, the military units in the northern sector took the bold step of surrendering. A task force of 150,000 soldiers and officers deserted their positions. The scene of thousands of unarmed men in uniform roaming the streets of Arbil, Sulaymaniyah and Dohuk was astounding. Kurdish families felt for these estranged and disillusioned soldiers and provided them with food and pocket money. Their commanders explained their position: Saddam's policies had wreaked havoc on the nation and humiliated the military. But they had no sense of direction. While they had been bold enough to defy military discipline, they were too timid to march on Baghdad and overthrow the regime. Their hesitation was best demonstrated by the fact that they deliberately rendered their weapons non-operational. This in itself was a brave and decisive step, as insubordination, desertion or mutiny was punishable by death. In the south, the military insurrection was one of desperation rather than a movement with clearly defined political aims. Both instances in the north and south reveal the extent to which the military had been de-politicised. Neither the Kurds in the north nor civilian Arab rebels in the south made any meaningful attempts to coordinate their rebellions with the military.

The third segment of the armed forces deployed in the middle sector of Iraq displayed the last trend – consistency and allegiance. Mainly composed of Republican Guard units, including the Madina, the Hammurabi and other armoured, mechanised and infantry divisions, these divisions were the major striking force of the regime. They had been kept in reserve to launch a counterattack, which never materialised. According to US General H. Norman Schwarzkopf, he was not given enough space to destroy these retreating Republican Guard divisions.[5] Unscathed, these divisions preyed on the scattered and lightly armed insurrections and ultimately saved the regime. The very section of the armed forces left intact by the Bush administration for Iraq's national defence carried out their domestic security tasks almost to perfection. The idea that these divisions remained loyal simply because they were better equipped and better paid stems largely from this and other minor experiences, above all the performance of Tawakalna Republican Guard division. Closer scrutiny reveals a host of other factors behind this cohesion. Firstly, the high density of kinship and party networks in the Republican Guard, when compared to the main army; secondly, they were unified by a sense of collective threat. This helped keep morale high and lent a sense of purpose and direction to the government's anti-revolt campaign. Finally, these high spirits were further enhanced by the relative safety of the Republican Guard's positions during the war. Having been withdrawn from Kuwait as soon as the air war started, they suffered few if any casualties.

These three contradictory trends, of mutiny, capitulation and cohesion, may well develop in the aftermath of any US invasion. The 1991 pattern was symmetrical, with each trend detectable in a specific sector. The pending campaign may encounter overlapping trends within each sector. Unlike the 1990–91 campaign, the battle lines may extend across the country, from south to north and west, cohesion or disintegration may well occur on both sides of the oversimplified dividing line between the main army and the Republican Guard.

The post-1991 reorganisation

From 1991 to 2001, the Iraqi regime carried out a restructuring strategy to put its ruling house and governmental institutions in order. This strategy involved: reorganising the ruling household, which was beginning to show signs of disunity; putting in place the arrangements for a smooth succession and forcing the re-tribalisation of society; and reorganising the military. These aspects were inter-linked and complementary.

On the first level, Saddam moved to reduce his over-reliance on his own house, the al-Majid. Instead he increasingly used his sub-clan, the albu Ghafour, which was formed from two houses: al-Majid and albu-Sultan. The former controls presidency and intelligence organs, the latter controls the army. Secondly, to avoid further friction, Saddam appointed his younger son, Qusay, as a successor. Qusay has since been nominated as a 'caretaker' and 'elected' to the party's regional command. Thirdly, Saddam set about reconstructing real and fictitious tribal groups. The aim of this was to compensate for the weakness of the party. Some tribes were empowered to administer justice and keep law and order; while others were entrusted with national security tasks, thus becoming an unofficial part of the armed forces. Lastly, the army was reorganised. In the previous 22 years (1968–90), there had only been four defence ministers. In less than six years (1991–96), there had been four reshuffles of the Ministry of Defence. Until 1996, the president had always kept the Ministry of Defence in the hands of al-Majid clan. In 1996, he changed direction and opted for a military veteran from the younger generation to satisfy the wider military establishment and tackle the problems of low morale. The present minister of defence, Thabit Sultan, was the result of this policy, chosen to replace the notorious Ali Hassan al-Majid, known to the Kurds as 'Chemical Ali' for his role in the attacks on Helabja.

The most far-reaching change was the drastic reduction in personnel. The armed forces were cut by almost one third (to an estimated 350,000). In terms of armaments, it was cut by roughly a half from its pre-1991 level. With the exception of air defence systems, this reduction in armaments has not seen an improvement in military hardware. However this downsizing has had positive effects for the regime. It helped create an economically sustainable institution and it raised the density of the kinship groups, which had become dangerously stretched in the pre-war one million-man army. The cleavage between the regular army and the elite formations was also enhanced. Numerically, the Republican Guard matches the regular army in terms of armed and mechanised divisions, lagging behind it only in terms of infantry divisions.

Today, the armed forces are organised in four rather than in two layers: the Special Republican Guard units, which are composed of a full corps with three divisions (other estimates put it at eight brigades); the Republican Guard, which includes three armoured divisions, one Mechanised Division (MD) and two Infantry Divisions (ID); the regular army, which consists of three Armoured Divisions (AD), three Mechanised Divisions (MD) and 11 Infantry Divisions (ID); and a layer of armed tribal units. They are in charge of quelling civilian disorder, but may offer a formidable force in any street combat.

The pending war

Compared to 1991, the nature of any possible war has changed in terms of political objectives, operational drive and battlefield zones. The political aspects of the campaign, as opposed to the sheer destructive force of coalition forces, will play a much larger part in shaping the attitude of the Iraqi military. This largely stems from the nature of the political system, the structure of the army and the stated aims of the pending war. As regime change is being overtly sought by the US, direct or proxy operations will have to culminate in taking the seat of power: Baghdad. If key Iraqi units are not won over or a coup successfully encouraged, then the main objective will be unattainable without full-scale invasion and occupation. This in turn would require the creation of a parallel administrative system across the whole of Iraq. The euphoria over the swift success in Afghanistan is misleading. Regime change in Iraq will not be technically or strategically straightforward.

Afghanistan and Iraq

Afghanistan does not prove the viability of enforced regime change in Iraq; rather it offers a classic anti-thesis. In the Afghani case, the US enterprise was anchored in a meticulous process that segregated the components of a nascent, simple political system. The Taliban movement was a small fundamentalist organisation with a core of religious zealots and a larger body of followers bound together by ideology, tribal solidarity and patronage or personal links. The Taliban regime had three major sources of power that were external to the regime. In addition to Saudi money (from Bin Laden and other sympathetic Saudi princes and officials), military and intelligence manpower from Pakistan formed the framework within which Taliban rule was built. A third supportive element was the tribal confederations, which have been the basis to the stability of Afghan regimes since independence in one of the least urbanised nations in the world.[6] These elements were well known to the US and easily targetable. A wealth of high-grade intelligence was available to the CIA from its own past involvement. This was enhanced by Pakistani and reported Iranian input. This allowed for the Afghani social and political landscape to be accurately mapped. Military action was thus launched on the basis of reliable and detailed information.

The first step was to dismantle the constituent parts of the Taliban's government, a relatively easy task. Diplomacy and political pressures removed Saudi financial support and Pakistani military support. Financial inducements were enough to remove the support of the tribal confederations. Depriving the Taliban of their three major sources of power reduced them to what they had originally been: a small and isolated radical religious movement. The US military campaign in Afghanistan went hand in hand with the wide-ranging political process which began at the Bonn conference. In the short term, this avoided the development of a political vacuum once the Taliban had been removed.

It is clear that Iraq is not Afghanistan. The components of the political system are much more complex and diverse. The political system in Iraq has been built over three decades. During this time it has been integrated into and come to dominate society. While this structure is not in the least monolithic, it still retains a strong cohesion and will offer much more resistance than the Taliban in Afghanistan.

A missing link: the political system

A comparative approach to Iraq and Afghanistan may prove far too tempting. To start with, the socio-political basis to the Iraqi regime is much more diverse, intertwined and complex. Unlike Afghanistan, the Iraqi state is a totalitarian system imposed on a mass urban society. Revived traditional tribalism and popular religion add to regime cohesion, but are not the basis to its power.

The Iraqi system uniquely combines aspects of a modern polity – mass politics, a command economy, oil rent and Arabist–Iraqi chauvinist–secular ideology – with tribal networks, kinship groups, Sufi orders and the discourse of traditional solidarities (*assabiya*). These Iraqi components are all domestically generated and have, since the 1970s, been skilfully blended. It is the relatively peaceful symbiosis of these elements that explains the regime's ability to survive thus far, but it is also an Achilles' heel.

Two sources of regime strength were crucial. The oil boom in the 1970s helped demobilise social forces and financed the massive security and war machines. Tribal affiliations added to the stability of the regime. In less than two decades, a sophisticated network of tribal alliances suffused the party, army, bureaucracy and business classes. Clans provided a core of lifetime kinship loyalties. Blood ties offered cohesive collective allegiances and manpower. Schisms within these clans did occur, in the leading tribe and indeed in its ruling house. But this offered Saddam Hussein another classic device, playing on inter-clan rivalries to rearrange internal power structures.

The result has been a semi-monolithic, extensive ruling group, enjoying hegemony over political power and wealth generation, and employing a varied and intertwined control system that manages both state and society. The 'ruling group' is better understood as a class-clan that permeates the army, party, intelligence services, bureaucracy and upper business class. At the core of this class-clan are the Beijat, with its leading house, the Albu Ghafour (comprising the al-Majid and Albu-Saltan extended families). The outer layers of this class-clan are mainly, but not exclusively, made up of a close-knit Sunni tribal alliance. Saddam Hussein is the president, the leader and the grand patriarch all in one.

This hybrid socio-political amalgam was built during the 1970s, fared well in the 1980s, but began to falter in the 1990s. The devastating effects of the two Gulf wars and the legacy of United Nations sanctions have disturbed peripheral elements of the system, but thus far never damaged its central core beyond repair. Blood ties, economic interests, and ideological and cultural bonds unite these groups, however alienated from the rest of the population they have become. An undifferentiated universal threat would serve only to repair potential and actual cleavages. This has been one of the weapons of mass integration deployed by the regime.

Breaking the unity of the ruling clan-class may prove to be a very difficult task. But the clan-class has to be divided before the armed forces lose their operational coherence. There is at the present time no apparent sign that the coherence of the ruling elite has been targeted. If and when certain segments of the ruling elite are neutralised or separated from the inner circle of the president, a reasonably controlled transition would have realistic chances of success. The possibilities for the disintegration of military units, irrespective of their insignia, may equally occur on both sides of the elite–general military divide.

The domestic politics of war

The regime in Baghdad is faced with two seemingly insurmountable problems. First, with the shift of US strategy under President George W. Bush, the nature of the pending conflict is totally different from 1990. Now, it is a war for survival and little else. Secondly, the divorce in Iraq over the last decade between official nationalism and popular patriotism seems irredeemable. While the two were united, the divisions between state and society could be hidden or at least dissipated. Now they are divided, widespread dissent and rebellion are much more likely.

An extensive survey conducted by the author in February–July 2002 suggests that Iraqis in the government controlled areas think the US has been conspiring to keep Saddam in place, to use his continued rule to frighten the Gulf States and increase the sale of armaments. On the other hand, Kurds fear Saddam Hussein's removal might not be swift enough to avoid his retaliation against them. They also fear one tyrant might replace another. There is, however, a grim awareness that the Iraqi army is no match for the US or a coalition of advanced armies.

So far the regime has tried to develop several remedies to the problems it faces. Firstly, there has been a strong tendency to manipulate and accentuate a sense of collective threat posed by the US to the whole of the ruling elite. The indiscriminate threat of elimination may well unite them and drive them to fight en masse to the bitter end. Ironically, this sense of collective vulnerability has been reinforced by the undifferentiated presentation of the objectives of the US campaign.

Secondly, to offset the inherent weakness of official nationalism, forms of popular and institutional religion have been mobilised. Anti-Shia communalism on the one hand, and Shi'ite religious rulings (*fatwa*) against the Shia opposition on the other, have been activated. This is a new mobilising device in lieu of nationalism proper.

Thirdly, the obvious military option pursued has been to fortify the cities as the best fighting locations. This may increase the possibilities of civilian casualties, slow down or limit US operations, offset the weakness of the Iraq army, and help achieve the regime's dream of inflicting as many US casualties as possible.

Fourthly, there is a careful plan to use the international media as much as possible, in the hope that this will pressure the attacking forces to stop short of Baghdad. In the desert there are few opportunities for sensational press coverage. In the 1991 Gulf War, the coalition forces controlled the media coverage. Now Iraq seems bent on reversing the situation. Ten radio stations have been installed in various underground locations.

Fifth, to ensure continuity, a bipolar system of political leadership has been created: Saddam and his son, Qusay, as the actual and reserve presidents. A third centre of power is also possible although it has not been announced: the commander of the Republican Army, General Kamal Mustafa.

Finally, to stem any potential mutiny by the public, military commanders have replaced civilian governors across Iraq. Loyal tribal forces are also to be deployed en masse in urban centres. These and other measures may reflect the extent to which the ruling elite is aware of its own weaknesses and of the possible limitations of the coalition camp.

Conclusion

Taking the 1991 experience as an example, the military on both sides of the major divide (mainstream army versus the Republican Guard) could fight, rebel or disintegrate. The possibilities will vary as events unfold across Iraq. The politics surrounding a possible coup are even more complicated. Compared to 1958, the military is today highly de-politicised. In 1958, one tenth of armed forces took part in the coup while at least 80% was neutralised by the swift takeover. In the present conditions, at least one fully-fledged corps (some 3–4 armed divisions) would be required, provided that the other three corps are politically neutralised. Without the cooperation of at least a considerable segment of the Beijat clan, such an eventuality is unthinkable. Whether or not the politics of the coalition campaign will succeed in attracting part of the ruling tribal alliance to their side is open to speculation. If, for whatever reason, a military coup failed, the possibilities of scattered and chaotic mutinies and the potential for a civil war would increase.

This paper relies heavily on some of my previous papers and monographs, among which are, Faleh A. Jabar, State and Civil Society in Iraq, *Ibn Khaldun Centre, Cairo, 1995 (in Arabic); (co-edited with Hisham Dawod)* Tribes and Power *(London: Saqi Books, 2002); 'Why the Uprisings Failed', in Fran Hazelton (ed.),* Iraq since the Gulf War, Prospects for Democracy *(London: ZED books, 1994); and 'State, Society, Clan, Party and Army in Iraq', in (edited with Ahmad Shikara and Keiko Sakai)* From Storm to Thunder, Unfinished Showdown Between Iraq and the US, *IDE Spot Survey, Institute for Developing Economies, Tokyo, 1998.*

Notes

1 This concept is widespread. It frequently occurs in media commentary, in statements made by politicians and, of course in research papers. See for example, Michael Eisenstadt, 'Like A Phoenix from the Ashes? The Future of Iraqi Military Power', The Washington Institute for Near East Policy, policy papers No. 36, 1993, p. 47 and 64. See also in this collection David Ochmanek's paper, 'A Possible US-Led Campaign Against Iraq: Key factors and an Assessment'.

2 *Revolutionary Iraq, 1968-1973,* The Political Report adopted by the Eight Regional Congress of the Arab Ba'th Socialist Party-Iraq, Baghdad, January, 1974, pp.135-136

3 There are three levels of party apprenticeship that precedes full membership: second degree advocate, *Naseer Thani,* first degree advocate, *Naseer Auwal,* and alternate member, *Murashah.*

4 Majid Khadduri, *Socialist Iraq: a study in Iraqi Politics Since 1968,* Middle East Institute, Washington, 1978, p.6 and 86.

5 General H. Norman Schwarzkopf with Peter Petrie, *It doesn't take a hero: the autobiography,* (London: Bantam Books, 1993).

6 Only 10% of the Afghan population are urban.

Chapter 7

The Kurdish Dilemma: The Golden Era Threatened

Gareth R. V. Stansfield

The two dominant political parties of Iraqi Kurdistan – the Kurdistan Democratic Party (KDP) and the Patriotic Union of Kurdistan (PUK) – face a dilemma. Before the events of 11 September 2001, the three northern governorates of Iraq (Dohuk, Arbil, Sulaymaniyah) remained free of the yoke of Baghdad, in effect benefiting from the events of 1991 that created a political vacuum within which an indigenous Kurdish political and administrative system emerged.[1] The situation was, and remains, highly anomalous. Iraqi Kurdistan was placed under double sanctions, one set from the UN that was imposed on the entirety of Iraq, the other from Saddam Hussein, who placed an internal embargo against the renegade region. The Kurds were protected by the efforts of *Operation Northern Watch* (the 'no-fly' zone), to guard them from the perceived aggression of Baghdad, yet military interventions from Iran and Turkey were seemingly tolerated. Within the parameters of external economic controls, political and military intervention and internal rivalry, the KDP and PUK, possibly by accident more than design, succeeded in heading an independent entity. After several rounds of conflict between the two parties, along with the involvement of other groups, Iraqi Kurdistan became divided in 1994 into two *de facto* 'statelets', each with its own

Kurdistan Regional Government (KRG) and each dominated by one of the two parties.

Both parties and, indeed, the Kurdish people as a whole accepted this situation. With sanctions seemingly keeping Saddam weakened, the oil-for-food deal (UN Resolution 986 and additions) providing the northern governorates with 13% of Iraqi oil revenue, together with the active smuggling of oil and other goods kept party coffers well endowed. With the PUK and KDP enjoying some form of international recognition granted by heading the *de facto* Kurdish governments in Arbil and Sulaymaniyah, the situation was acceptable for all concerned. Saddam remained a threat, but he was a threat the Kurds could live with, particularly from 1997 onwards.[2]

The eleventh of September changed the delicate balance which had kept the Kurds safe in their geopolitical anomaly. For the leadership of the Iraqi opposition in general, it was readily apparent and indeed hoped for that the regime of Saddam Hussein would be implicated, sooner rather than later, in the terrorist attacks. However, more than any other Iraqi opposition party, the KDP and PUK have a great deal to lose. As the geopolitical gaze of George W Bush turned towards Iraq, the KDP and PUK were well aware that the political gains made since 1991, the economic benefits made available to them and the fragile but real security they enjoyed, were threatened by a possible change in the status quo.

The Kurds since 1991

After the Kurdish *rapareen* (uprising) and the withdrawal of central government institutions in 1991 from Iraqi Kurdistan, multi-party elections were held in May 1992, returning a Kurdistan National Assembly (KNA) equally divided between the KDP and PUK. The executive KRG reflected this division and adopted a system of power-sharing of ministerial positions for the first and second cabinets.[3] However, the absence of both Massoud Barzani and Jalal Talabani from positions of leadership within the newly formed government and the interference of neighbouring countries stoking the volatile rivalry that was ever present between the KDP and PUK resulted in the collapse of the unified KRG and the start of interfactional fighting in 1994. The PUK occupied the regional capital, Arbil, with the KDP retaining control of the revenue-generating areas of Dohuk and Zakho.

Political development

By the mid-1990s, tensions had reached new highs. Both the KDP and PUK were active participants within Iraqi opposition groups, most notably the Iraqi National Congress (INC), yet the KDP and PUK remained rivals. Their attitudes toward the INC reflect this rivalry. The PUK maintained strong links with the INC and its nominal leader, Dr Ahmed Chalabi, while the KDP took a more cautious approach. The differences in this relationship were highlighted by the INC-PUK operation conducted against Saddam's northern forces in March 1995.[4] The PUK was a full partner in the venture, which ultimately failed after US support did not materialise. The KDP, however, remained wary, did not commit troops, and attempted to prevent the attack from taking place. From its perspective, caution was essential. Recognising its weak position in Iraq and its vulnerability to an Iraqi assault, Massoud Barzani adopted a position that would keep the KDP and KDP-administered areas safe whilst guaranteeing the failure of the planned INC-PUK assault, demonisation of PUK leader Jalal Talabani in Baghdad and damaging Ahmed Chalabi's credibility in the US. For the PUK and INC, it was the start of a tortured five-year period that saw their expulsion from Arbil by Saddam's forces in August 1996 and the marginalisation of the INC.[5] In 1995 and 1996, the strategy of maintaining cautious ties to the US while maintaining links with Baghdad proved successful. Today, this careful distance from the US is proving to be less effective in protecting KDP interests.

Since 1996, two *de facto* entities have therefore existed side-by-side, each with its own government, each with a dominant political party and each claiming to represent the Kurdish people.[6] Yet the level of tension between them has decreased markedly. Whether this is due to the parties' territorial separation, or the hands-off posture of formerly meddlesome neighbours who do not – for the moment – view a divided Kurdistan as a threat, is hard to tell. Both factors are probably at work. US policy aimed at promoting KDP-PUK unification at this time, however, might inadvertently spur competition and even open conflict and increase the temptation of neighbouring states to heighten intra-Kurdish tensions.[7]

Economic development

Since 1997 and the implementation of the oil-for-food deal, Iraqi

Kurdistan has enjoyed economic prosperity and, arguably, a certain amount of political liberalisation.[8] Through this allocation of revenue, Iraqi Kurdish society has changed significantly. From being perhaps the most underdeveloped region of the country in the 1960s and 1970s, and suffering the effects of one of the most brutal military operations launched by a state against its own citizens in the 1980s, Iraqi Kurdistan has managed to advance since the withdrawal of Saddam's government in 1991 and is now the most economically prosperous portion of the country. UN surveys have indicated that child mortality is lower in Iraqi Kurdistan than in the centre and south of Iraq. Increased disposable income has further fuelled economic expansion in the service sector and in the sale of expensive consumer products and high-tech equipment. New economic actors – entrepreneurs, factory owners, small businessmen – have emerged as a result. Preserving the economic and social conditions that have nourished these developments will be key to stability during and after a transitional period. Economic prosperity and the encouragement of a freer economy by the dominant parties, whether by accident or design, is replenishing the depleted middle and mercantile classes. Economic advancement rather than the lure of the militia and Kurdish nationalism is what tends to occupy young Kurds today, particularly in the urban centres.[9]

The oil-for-food programme has acted as a catalyst in the institutionalisation of the Kurdish Regional Governments (KRGs) in Arbil and Sulaymaniyah. The Kurdish authorities collaborate closely with the UN agencies administering the programme and have a significant responsibility in constructing the distribution plans for each phase. Kurdish civil servants have also been consistently exposed to UN operating procedures and benefited from a range of training programmes designed by UN agencies and NGOs. The result is an increasingly active civil service in the three major cities (Dohuk, Arbil and Sulaymaniyah) as the UN operates according to a governorate division, assisting in the formation of a skilled body of bureaucrats. Futhermore, the existence of the KRGs for over a decade has institutionalised the structure of Kurdish governance in the minds of the population. Kurds in their early 20s now struggle to remember what life was like under the Ba'ath regime and associate the word 'government' with Kurdish rather than Iraqi rule.

The durability of these gains will depend on getting two

things right. The first will be to ensure that the income now deriving from oil revenue is not cut off. Since 1998, 13% of Iraq's oil revenue has been allocated to the northern governorates of Iraq under UNSCR. Apart from its immediate financial benefits, this arrangement has brought Kurdish civil servants directly into contact with UN and NGO counterparts, thereby promoting the bureaucratic development of the Kurdish administration, and has promoted the development of a range of local NGOs, the presence of which will be vital in a post-Saddam Iraq. This revenue has lubricated relations between the KDP and PUK by reducing the imbalance of funds available to the two parties and their respective administrations. With its control of the lucrative border crossings at Zakho, the KDP has, until recently, been able to generate significant sums through trade between Iraq and Turkey. The amounts vary, although estimates of several hundred thousand dollars per week would appear to be conservative. The PUK, with its crossings on the Iranian border, has not been able to generate equivalent sums, resulting in the advancement of the KDP in economic and military terms from 1996 onwards. Indeed, the PUK attack on the KDP in 1997 was as a direct consequence of this imbalance, and the struggle for resources remained volatile until the 13% of UN-derived revenue became available.

The second issue will be to ensure that the effect of monetary unification in the wake of a war does not have a sharply negative effect on Iraqi Kurdistan. The Kurdish-controlled region of Iraq now uses the Old Iraqi Dinar (OID), which exchanges at approximately 12 OID to US$1. It is a reasonably stable currency, but is honoured only in the north. In contrast, the New Iraqi Dinar (NID) circulated by the government in Baghdad has been greatly devalued by inflation, trading at 3,000 NID to US$1. Thinking should begin now about the basis on which the OID will be exchanged for the NID when transitional authorities begin the task of integrating the northern economy into the national economy in a post-war period.

The Kurdish political strategy since 11 September 2001
The Kurds and the US
The KDP and PUK represent perhaps the most militarily powerful force in the opposition to Saddam, along with the Shia Supreme Council for Islamic Revolution in Iraq (SCIRI). In an attempt to

capitalise on this, and the fact that the KDP and PUK control a vast swathe of Iraq between them, the two parties promoted themselves as something akin to the Northern Alliance of Afghanistan throughout early 2002. Their aim was to strengthen their position with the US in anticipation of regime change. It was an unworkable strategy. Turkey would not allow the Kurds to play a crucial role in a war and the US is unlikely to grant the KDP and PUK a role similar to that of the Northern Alliance in Afghanistan, if only because the *peshmerga* are so weak relative to regime forces. Thus, the KDP, and to a lesser extent the PUK, now face two problems: the marginalisation of their influence after the war – stemming in part from the small role they will have in the fighting – and the reversion to the central government of the oil revenues they now enjoy. For the KDP, this problem will be complicated by the closure of the illegal oil smuggling route from Mosul through KDP territory at Dohuk and into Turkey, which now generates considerable revenue. Both parties are aware of their dilemma and are working assiduously to maintain a high profile in Washington and secure as many guarantees as possible from the US before regime change has been realised. Their actions reflect a higher degree of political sophistication and awareness than we have witnessed previously. As usual, however, the PUK and KDP are pursuing the same objective in different and not always complementary ways.

The Kurds and the Iraqi opposition

As Judith Yaphe notes in this volume, along with the Shia, Kurds are the traditional war-fighters of the Iraqi opposition.[10] Furthermore, Kurds provide the opposition movement with territorial legitimacy and the moral high ground, given atrocities committed by Saddam against the Iraqi Kurds. The KDP and PUK are able to field approximately 80,000 *peshmerga* and armed troops between them.[11] Currently, without Kurdish support, no grouping of Iraqi opposition parties (whether it be the INC, the 'Gang of Four' or the 'Group of Six') can operate effectively or exercise a decisive influence on US decision-makers. The KDP and PUK have attempted to capitalise on their salience in advance of a war, aware that once the action starts their ability to influence their situation will wane. However, whilst on the surface it may seem that the KDP and PUK operate closely within the Iraqi opposition setting, their methods differ.

Despite their superficial cooperation within the opposition, the Kurds remain divided, whatever pronouncements emerge from Sulaymaniyah or Salahadin regarding the potential unification of the Kurdish political system. But with the US focus on regime change in Iraq, the internal differences have been put aside for the foreseeable future. Still, this inherent rivalry has resulted in different positions being staked out within the Iraqi opposition movement.

The KDP's support for the overall Iraqi opposition has changed depending upon international circumstances. The overriding aim of the party has been to maintain stability in its area of Iraqi Kurdistan at any cost, and it adapts its policies to this broad goal. The result has been heightened prosperity for Arbil and Dohuk governorates, and, of course, for the KDP itself, but it has, at times, seriously weakened the opposition movement.

The KDP withdrawal from the INC–PUK revolt in 1995 and its alliance with Baghdad in 1996 illustrate the party's 'no permanent enemies, only permanent interests' approach to Kurdish politics. In the latter episode, the combined forces of the Iraqi military and the KDP swept through PUK-occupied Arbil, forcing out the PUK and capturing several hundred INC militia, who were executed by the occupying Iraqi forces. The INC was devastated. It lost its bases in Iraqi Kurdistan, many of its activists were killed and Saddam had secured a major propaganda victory. The PUK, similarly, was severely weakened. For the KDP, however, it was the start of a five-year period of unrivalled prosperity for Arbil, Dohuk and the KDP itself, and an increase in overall security. It is the maintenance of this position which now dominates the thinking of the KDP, and which has meant that, at times, Barzani and the KDP leadership have remained somewhat aloof from the activities of the rest of the opposition.

For the PUK, it has been easier to deal with the Iraqi opposition due to its long-standing relations with the INC, greater economic security and Talabani's openly bombastic attitude towards Saddam. Talabani tends to seize opportunities as they appear. Sometimes this works (he certainly looks successful at the end of 2002) and sometimes he loses badly (as in his misjudged attack against the KDP in 1997). He is also much less cautious than Barzani. They both understand the American message, but instead of erring with Barzani on the side of caution, Talabani has gone out of his way to 'make the right noises' in the US. The PUK has avoided aggravating the Turkish government, which would place the US in a difficult position; and, perhaps most importantly, it has attempted to become politically essential to the Iraqi opposition.

The KDP fully appreciates the determination of the US administration to remove Saddam's regime. However, whilst the KDP leadership's opposition towards Saddam is unequalled, it can be argued that Saddam has proved to be a more reliable ally in times of need than the US.[12] The invasion of Arbil in August 1996 illustrates this fact, and the shared economic interests between the KDP and Baghdad are readily apparent. The KDP, which has nurtured its position, particularly since 1997, and become perhaps the most powerful entity in Iraqi Kurdistan, has more to lose in a post-Saddam Iraq than the PUK. The KDP, therefore, is aggressively pursuing a federal Kurdish entity within a new Iraq in an attempt to preserve its pre-eminence. Virtually all calls for 'federalism' have originated from the KDP, as have recent attempts to unify the political system.[13] The KDP's relations with Turkey have deteriorated as KDP rhetoric has become increasingly nationalistic (particularly when the issue of the Turkoman population is brought up by Ankara as a means to allow proxy intervention).

The approach of the PUK is somewhat different. Talabani still espouses a federal model for a post-Saddam Iraq, but not as vociferously as the KDP. When necessary, the PUK seems content to play down Kurdish nationalism and instead pursue a policy of unfettered collaboration with the Iraqi opposition as a whole, refusing to become embroiled in issues relating to the Turkomans or the details of a federal system.

The KDP and PUK are attempting to secure their objectives for a post-Saddam Iraq whilst Saddam is still in power. It is a dangerous game, but one that they have to play. Only time will tell which strategy will prove to be successful – the cooperative and pro-opposition approach of the PUK or the cautious yet nationalistic style of the KDP. Perhaps the next round of these strategies will be played out in the forthcoming conference of Iraqi opposition groups. If we consider the major gatherings of the opposition which have occurred since 1991 – in Vienna (June 1992), Salahadin (October 1992) and New York (October 1999) – the Kurds have always managed to achieve concessions on different aspects of Kurdish interests, whether they be national rights, federalism or inclusion in central government.

The influence of outside actors

There has been a dangerous propensity for the KDP and PUK to encourage neighbouring states to become involved in the internal affairs of Iraqi Kurdistan. The three countries which could possibly become involved during the process of regime change are Iran, Turkey and, of course, Iraq itself. A further dynamic, which has been developing steadily since late 1998, is the influence of al-Qaeda upon Iraqi Kurdistan's indigenous Islamist groups.

Current regional relations

The political geography of Iraqi Kurdistan has resulted in the KDP and PUK forming different sets of relations with neighbouring states. The KDP, with its long border with Turkey, has had for the most part a fruitful partnership with its powerful northern neighbour. Both Turkey and the KDP benefited from huge amounts of oil being smuggled from Mosul (Iraq-proper) into KDP territory at Dohuk and Zakho, and then into Turkey. The KDP also assisted Turkish forces in targeting Kurdistan Workers' Party (PKK) forces based in Iraqi Kurdistan in the mid-1990s, and Turkey came to Massoud Barzani's aid when the PUK attacked the KDP in 1997.[14] More recently, however, the relationship has become increasingly acrimonious. Fuelled by the KDP's use of the rhetoric of Kurdish nationalism and its active advancement of a federal Kurdish entity in Iraq with Kirkuk at its centre, Turkey has significantly reduced the oil-smuggling revenue and has adopted in other ways a threatening posture towards the KDP. Turkey has proved to be particularly adept at using the Iraqi Turkoman Front (ITF) as a proxy against Barzani, further fuelling tensions.[15]

PUK-controlled territory shares a long border with Iran, and the PUK has always relied upon Tehran for support. More recently, however, strains were created by Iran's policy of protecting and supporting the various Islamist groups which operate east of Sulaymaniyah in the environs of Halabja, Khormal and Tawella. The PUK and Islamists have fought in the past, and the activities of groups such as Ansar al-Islam, which have included the assassination of a leading KDP politician, Franso Hariri, and the attempted assassination of the PUK Prime Minister Dr Barham Saleh, have led Talabani to take an increasingly coercive line against Ansar.[16] But, probably due to Iranian pressure, the PUK has still not managed to fully remove the threat posed by these groups.[17] Perhaps for this reason, from 2000 onwards, the PUK actively courted Turkey as a potential ally. Relations between the two had previously been strained by the PUK's tacit support of the PKK and by the Turkish military supporting the KDP in 1997. However, by 2001, the Turkey-PUK relationship was strong and the PUK had seemingly achieved what many thought to be impossible – cooperating with the governments of Turkey and Iran simultaneously.

Kurdish-inspired involvement

Would the Kurds themselves invite a neighbouring power into Iraqi Kurdistan during the regime-change period? Such events have not been uncommon over the last ten years, whether it has been the PUK seeking Iranian involvement or the KDP seeking Turkish or Iraqi intervention. The situation is now quite different. The heightened determination of the US to remove Saddam would make the chances of either the KDP or PUK inviting a neighbouring country's intervention remote. Both parties have learnt that they do not benefit from encouraging external intervention into their affairs, and that short-term gains can have damaging long-term consequences. However, their ability to resist the pressure which countries such as Iran and Turkey can apply, let alone the regime of Saddam Hussein, is questionable. If these parties were faced with a situation that could spell their ultimate demise, for example, the removal of the allocation of Iraqi oil revenue for the Kurdish region or the limiting of domestic political power, then the result would be political instability with a range of consequences, one of which could be a call for outside intervention.

Turkish and Iranian involvement

The leaderships of both KDP and PUK covet Kirkuk as the 'jewel in the crown' of Iraqi Kurdistan. However, there is probably no other event which would mobilise Turkey towards military intervention than Kirkuk being in the hands of Jalal Talabani or Massoud Barzani. This may be considered a product of the Iraqi Kurdistan of the period 1960–90, when Kirkuk was the holy grail, the city of Kurdish folklore, for the guerrillas and *peshmerga*. The issue of Kirkuk has been heavily politicised recently, and again reflects the different approaches of the KDP and PUK to the current predicament. In brief, the Turkish government has been keen to portray Kirkuk as a Turkoman city, rather than Kurdish. The KDP response has been one of promoting the overt 'Kurdishness' of Kirkuk and disparaging the Iraqi Turkoman community in Iraqi Kurdistan as a whole, thereby again heightening tensions with Ankara. The PUK, however, has been blurring the issue of Kirkuk, with Barham Saleh indicating that perhaps the Turkish government was correct, a statement that provoked a furious exchange of views between the PUK and hard-line Kurdish nationalists.

Neither the KDP nor the PUK will ever really relinquish their desire to possess Kirkuk. The events of 1991 demonstrate the ability of the two parties to infiltrate an area and provoke an uprising. As Kirkuk is the only city worthy of such an effort from the Kurdish perspective, it would be surprising if arrangements were not in hand to start a revolt when the opportunity arises.

Iran's military interventions into Iraqi Kurdistan after the Iran–Iraq War have been far more limited than those of Turkey. Since the 1990s, its interventions have usually been limited and in support of its Kurdish ally, the PUK. Iran has used Iraqi Kurdish territory to support Islamist groups (especially around Halabja), or to pressure Saddam's regime by inserting elements of the SCIRI Badr Army into Kurdish territory. Iran would intervene if the formation of an Iraqi Kurdish 'state' was on the horizon, which is unlikely, or if Turkish influence increased dramatically. The disposition of Kirkuk would be important, because a long-term Kurdish occupation of Kirkuk would encourage a Turkish intervention, which would push Iran into a similar venture. This is yet another reason why Kirkuk remains a highly dangerous variable in a regime change scenario and explains the emphasis that US military planning gives to 'the race for Kirkuk.'

Both Turkey and Iran have their proxies within Iraqi Kurdistan. For Turkey, the Turkoman population has been politicised and presents a significant problem for Massoud Barzani and the KDP. Turkey is also promoting the interests of the ITF to the US administration, and it is highly probable that it will achieve increased prominence among the Iraqi opposition groups as a result, much to the consternation of the KDP. For Iran, the various Islamist groups which are present in Iraqi Kurdistan are an obvious conduit by which to influence the political affairs of the region. The growing militancy of these groups and their alleged links with al-Qaeda are receiving an increasing amount of attention from US and other Western government agencies.

Political Islam and al-Qaeda activity in Iraqi Kurdistan[18]

Iraqi Kurdistan is a predominantly Islamic society, and it should therefore be no surprise that there has been a steady development of Islamist political parties in the region, particularly since 1991.[19] Some of these parties, including the Islamic Movement of Kurdistan (IMK) had formed as early as the late 1970s, sparked by the Islamic Revolution in Iran and had fought against Saddam's regime during the 1980s.[20] However, it was the development of the *de facto* state and the instabilities which characterised Iraqi Kurdistan in the mid-1990s that gave Islamist parties the space and opportunity in which to become a force in the region.

The IMK, under the leadership of Sheikh Othman Abdel Aziz, benefited from a series of defectors from the KDP and PUK ranks. The defectors had became increasingly despondent due to the interfactional fighting prevalent in the early to mid-1990s. The ranks of the IMK were further swelled by returning Kurds who had fought with the *mujahiddin* in Afghanistan. From early 1992, according to PUK sources, Saddam established links with the IMK, authorising his security network to fund and provide equipment to it in order to promote instability in Iraqi Kurdistan. The IMK was therefore in a position to benefit from the support of both Iran and Iraq.

The IMK subsequently became embroiled in the interfactional fighting which broke out in 1994. Serious fighting between the IMK and PUK took place throughout the region. After being severely weakened by the PUK, the IMK benefited from the action of the KDP and Iraqi government against the PUK in August 1996 and succeeded in achieving control of the Halabja region and areas bordering with Iran. From 1997, an uneasy peace existed between the PUK and IMK. However, throughout this period, the IMK was being increasingly radicalised by Kurds returning from Afghanistan, and by the movement of support away from Sheikh Othman's replacement, his brother Mulla Ali Abdel Aziz, towards a younger and more militant range of party leaders. Mulla Ali attempted to stem these developments by amalgamating the IMK with the Islamic Renaissance Party (IRP), headed by his brother, Mulla Siddiq, to form the Islamic Unity Movement of Kurdistan (IUMK), but it proved to be too late.

Chief among the younger leaders within the Islamist movements was Mulla Ali Bapir. On 30 May 2002, Ali Bapir declared the establishment of the Islamic Group of Kurdistan (IGK), effectively breaking up the IMK. Ali Bapir attracted approximately three-quarters of IUMK personnel and achieved control of the Iran–Iraq border area. At the same meeting which saw the establishment of the IGK, the ultra-fanatical members demanded a *jihad* to be launched, particularly against the secularist KDP and PUK. Mulla Ali and Ali Bapir both refused, resulting in a further split and the formation of the Jund al-Islam on 31 August 2001. According to PUK sources, Osama bin Laden stepped into this division and supported the unification of the more extreme Islamist Kurdish groups previously marginalised by the IUMK. The main militant groups with significant numbers of Kurds who had fought in Afghanistan were as follows: Kurdish Hamas, formed in 1997 by Omar Barziyani due to his disapproval of the IMK-PUK peace process; Islamic Tawhid, created covertly in Arbil as a sub-group of IMK, headed by Mulla Salman al-Tawhidi; and the Hezi Du Soran (Soran Second Force). This was the largest army of the IUMK, consisting of some 400 highly trained Kurdish fighters complemented by some 60 Arab-Afghans. The force was commanded by Aso Hawleri.

The Jund al-Islam was renamed Ansar al-Islam after Najmuddin Faraj Ahmad (Mulla Krekar) took a leadership role. Mulla Krekar was previously a military commander under Mulla Ali Abdel Aziz in the IUMK. He attempted to be a moderating influence, in relative terms, upon the Ansar al-Islam and pursued a policy of attempting to work towards a reconciliation with the PUK and promoting relations with the KRG in Sulaymaniyah. His arrest in the Netherlands in September 2002 may shed some light on the more secretive influences which permeate the militant Islamist groups within Iraqi Kurdistan.[21] It appears that Saddam's security apparatus and the network of al-Qaeda have both been involved with Kurdish Islamist groups. However, whether this involvement occurred concomitantly and in a coordinated manner still remains unclear.

Conclusion

The problem the Kurds face is that, once Saddam is removed, their position on the international stage weakens. They have to attempt to locate themselves in positions of influence and authority with the US and within the Iraqi opposition. The KDP, keen to preserve its position of dominance, is pursuing a policy which may be characterised as cautious towards the US (thereby hedging its bets with Saddam, just in case), domineering within the opposition (in an attempt to create an opposition in which its influence is maximised), and confrontational towards Turkey (a manifestation of its Kurdish nationalism). The PUK, starting from a weaker position, recognises that it could benefit greatly from regime change and, therefore, is more open towards US objectives cooperative within the opposition (as a means to achieve influence in a future Baghdad), and is attempting to keep relations with all neighbours problem-free.

In the event of a military attack aimed at regime change, the most immediate concern would be the fate of Kirkuk. It is the tripwire which could promote external involvement from Turkey and then Iran, and could also witness fighting between different ethnic groups (whether they be Kurd, Turkomen or indeed Arab), or even between the KDP and PUK themselves. In the transitional period, immediate concerns would include maintaining the value of the Kurdish unit of currency, the OID, and the provisions made for maintaining the share of oil revenue for the northern governorates.

Kurdish politicians from every party constantly use the phrase the 'Kurdish genie is now out of the bottle', meaning that it will be impossible for the Kurds to return to their former victimised, marginalised position. But they may be wrong. If Saddam is removed, the focus of the world in general, and the US administration in particular, will be on Baghdad. Saddam will probably be replaced by a Sunni Arab politician, and the international community will concentrate upon rehabilitating the Iraqi economy and reintegrating it, and its oil wealth, into the international system. By then, the danger is that the Kurds' voice will be still heard, but rarely listened to. The leaderships of KDP and the PUK will have to ensure that they speak with a unified voice and act in a unified manner in an attempt to keep the gains that have been made.

Notes

1 For the purposes of this paper, the northern governorates of Iraq, which have been outside the control of Baghdad since 1991, are referred to as 'Iraqi Kurdistan'. This is not to imply that the region is wholly 'Kurdish'. There are significant populations of other peoples, including Assyrians and Turkomans. Furthermore, the area of the region in Iraq which may be identified as possessing a majority Kurdish population is somewhat greater than 'Iraqi Kurdistan' as defined.

2 1997 was the year in which the last round of fighting between the KDP and PUK occurred. Since then, a ceasefire has been maintained and an attempt has been made to implement normalisation strategies as agreed in the US-brokered Washington Agreement of September 1998.

3 The prime minister of the first cabinet (June 1992–March 1993) was Dr Fuad Massoum of the PUK, with Dr Roj Nuri Shawais of the KDP appointed as deputy prime minister. The second cabinet (March 1993–August 1996) was presided over by Kosrat Rasoul Ali of the PUK, again with Dr Roj as Deputy. The KDP headed the KNA with Jawher Namiq Salim being appointed Speaker.

4 The attack aimed to destroy the Iraqi V Corps stationed at the Iraqi–Kurdish dividing line, capture Mosul and Kirkuk and promote a national uprising against Saddam.

5 The situation between the KDP and PUK continued to worsen throughout 1995 and 1996. The KDP was angered by its expulsion from Arbil and concerned about the increasing militarisation of the PUK. The PUK continued to be motivated by gaining a share of the ever-increasing oil-smuggling revenue which the KDP received through its control of Dohuk and Zakho. Recognising these problems, neighbouring countries were heavily involved in the heightening of tension, with Iran supporting the PUK, and the KDP increasingly turning to Baghdad. Claiming concern regarding the strength of the PUK-Iran alliance in mid-1996, and receiving little support from the US to alleviate the problem, the KDP formed a temporary alliance with Saddam, resulting in the invasion of Arbil city and the expulsion of the PUK.

6 The KDP and PUK agreed to re-assemble a joint KNA in Arbil in October 2002, with PUK representatives taking their places for the first time since the invasion of Arbil in August 1996. The reunification of the KNA was called for by the Washington Agreement of 1998 and it is thought that the US has applied pressure to unite the Kurds in advance of regime change in Iraq. Yet it is more likely that the initiative originated with the PUK and KDP themselves, as the Washington Agreement has been increasingly overlooked by the US as it focuses more on Baghdad. It is, however, highly likely that the full unification of the Kurdish political system, with a unified executive, will be overtaken by events.

7 Since 1996, Kurdish-controlled Iraq has been divided into two administrative areas, each

representing the area of dominance of the KDP and PUK. The KDP retain the entirety of the governorate of Dohuk, with most of Arbil governorate, including the capital city of Arbil itself. The KDP therefore occupies the northwestern portion of Iraqi Kurdistan, with its KRG residing in Arbil and the KDP headquarters nearby in Salahadin. The PUK retains the entirety of the governorate of Sulaymaniyah, with a large portion of Kirkuk governorate (though not including the city of Kirkuk itself), and a small part of Arbil governorate. The PUK's governmental apparatus resides in the city of Sulaymaniyah, with its party structure being divided between this city and the political bureau complex at Kalarcholan.

8   The original oil-for-food deal (Security Council Resolution 986) was agreed between the government of Iraq and the UN in 1996. However, it was not until 1997 that funds became available through the programme.

9   Iraqi Kurdistan now has a predominantly urban population, with an overall estimated population of approximately 4 million people.

10 Yaphe, J (2002) 'America's War on Iraq: Myths and Opportunities', in this volume.

11 It is useful to make a distinction between the *peshmerga* and the 'Kurdistan Army'. The *peshmerga* remain the traditional tribal militia of the KDP and the older informal militia of the PUK. Both parties have attempted to rationalise their military structures and place military activities under the control of their respective KRGs and Ministry of *Peshmerga* Affairs (Defence). There are therefore party *peshmerga* (normally the 'old guard' of the Kurdish movement) and 'government' soldiers (mainly recruited in the post-1996 period).

12 Arguably, few families/tribes have been targeted as systematically as the Barzanis by Saddam's regime.

13 The KDP went as far as creating a 'draft constitution for an Arab-Kurdish federation in Iraq'. The document was then accepted by the PUK towards the end of September 2002. Federalism has become a dominant theme of the KDP's media outlets, and has been forwarded extensively by the Centre for Global Peace at the American University in Washington DC, where the KDP funds the Mulla Mustafa Barzani Chair (see, for example, Carole O'Leary, 'Post-Saddam Iraq', *Washington Times*, 26 September 2002).

14 The PKK (Parti Karkaren Kurdistan – Kurdistan Workers' Party), is a Turkish Kurdish separatist party headed, until his capture, by Abdullah Ocalan.

15 A common strategy employed by the ITF has been to pay Iraqi Kurds to register as Turkomans, thereby officially increasing the proportion of Turkomans within the region. The presence of this Turkic minority in the region is used, in part, to justify Turkish military intervention in Iraqi Kurdistan.

16 Franso Hariri, close confidante of Massoud Barzani, ex-governor of Arbil and head of the KDP's Arbil party organisation, was

assassinated in February 2001 by groups reportedly affiliated to the renegade al-Tawhid faction of the Islamic Unity Movement of Kurdistan (IUMK). Barham Saleh survived an assassination attempt in April 2002. His assailants were captured and admitted to belonging to the Jund al-Islam (later renamed Ansar al-Islam).

[17] The PUK is adamant that these groups are part of, or at least related to, the al-Qaeda network, and have as members certain high ranking Arab-Afghans of that organisation. The leader of one of the main groups, Mulla Krekar of the Ansar al-Islam, was arrested in the Netherlands on 13 September 2002. It remains to be seen whether links between Kurdish Islamist groups and al-Qaeda will be verified.

[18] The focus of this section is on the more militant Islamist factions of Iraqi Kurdistan. It is important to note that there are several moderate Islamist parties, charities and groups that operate in the region and are a force promoting stability. The most prominent of these groups is the Kurdistan Islamic Union (KIU), which adheres to a policy of unarmed political activity and full involvement with all political parties and the KRGs. Interestingly, the KIU is the most popular Islamist political party in Iraqi Kurdistan and may prove to be a significant actor if democratic structures are developed further in the region. The KIU is part of the Muslim Brotherhood and has been supported to a significant extent by Saudi Arabia and other Gulf states.

[19] Sources for this section include interviews conducted in Halabja with members of Islamist parties and discussions with PUK personnel in Sulaymaniyah. Information regarding the historical development of militant Islamist parties in Iraqi Kurdistan has been provided by Roj Nariman Bahjat (a KRG-PUK official in Sulaymaniyah during 1999–2001), who conducted field research in Iraqi Kurdistan during the rise of the Jund al-Islam.

[20] Interview with IMK Political Bureau members, Halabja, June 1998.

[21] His arrest was made possible due to the fact that Iran refused him entry, possibly in an attempt to placate the US in the current focus on Islamist militant groups. He then landed in Sweden which handed him over to Dutch authorities on drug trafficking charges. US administration representatives are reportedly very keen to interview him.

Chapter 8

Economy and Society in Iraqi Kurdistan: Fragile Institutions and Enduring Trends

Michiel Leezenberg

Due to internal and external factors, Iraqi Kurdistan has not developed into a stable political entity; consequently, its political future is all the more uncertain. Whatever action the US will eventually decide to take against Iraq, one thing is absolutely clear: the fate of the Iraqi Kurds will be contingent on developments concerning the country as a whole. Given the importance of events beyond the control of those in Iraqi Kurdistan, this paper will focus on the extent to which the current social and economic conditions of the region are solid enough to survive any dramatic political developments; and to a lesser extent on the question of whether the region's experience of the past ten years may serve as a model for a possible future democratisation of Iraq.

Clientelisation and civil society
After ten years of *de facto* Kurdish self-rule, Iraqi Kurdistan has experienced moderate economic prosperity, but little durable political stability. It is true that despite the shortcomings of the Kurdish parties, the region is in most respects far better off under Kurdish rule than it has ever been under the Ba'ath government; but these achievements are under the permanent threat of disruptive

outside intervention, be it from the Iraqi government and military, or from other countries, most importantly, Turkey and Iran. The ever-increasing likelihood of an American military operation against Iraq has made both the Iraqi Kurds and their neighbours rather nervous, and triggered intensive diplomatic activity.

The effects of outside interference have been aggravated by the behaviour of the two main Kurdish parties: the Kurdish Democratic Party (KDP) and the Patriotic Union of Kurdistan (PUK). In 1992, a promising first move towards democratisation was made by the organisation of local elections, but there was no adequate follow-up to this effort. Instead, for several years, the parties were locked in bloody internecine fighting. Since 1998, a process of normalisation has been ongoing, but neither of the parties has seemed very eager to give up on its present privileges in exchange for a return to parliamentary rule. It was only the prospect of an impending American action and increasingly martial language from Turkey that pressured the Kurdish leadership into reconvening the regional parliament, something they had not been able to achieve in four years of negotiations and confidence-building measures.

There have been serious efforts at the imposition of civilian government and the rule of law in Iraqi Kurdistan, but these have been hampered, not only by the lack of international political support, but also by the refusal of the leaders of both the KDP and the PUK, Massoud Barzani and Jalal Talabani, to become part of the elected structures. In May 1992, elections for a regional government were held; these elections were carefully set up in such a way as to work within the parameters of the 1974 autonomy law that was meant to have given more power to the Kurds to administer their own region. The elections of 1992 were remarkably free and fair, certainly by regional standards. The parliament and government that were subsequently formed, however, were divided up according to a strict 50–50 division of ministerial posts and other resources. In a move that undermined the government, the leaders of the KDP and PUK Massoud Barzani and Jalal Talabani, failed to join either the parliament or the government. This meant that the parties, and especially the party politbureaus, continued to exercise effective political power. Added to this was the fact that the government itself had a budget that was smaller than that of either KDP or PUK, as well as that of the numerous foreign aid organisations working in the Kurdish enclave. It became clear that the government's political authority and economic influence were severely restricted from the start.

Instead of leading to the development of government institutions that were independent of the KDP and PUK, the 50–50 division exacerbated existing patterns of patronage. Both parties, as well as numerous other local organisations, engaged in serious attempts at clientelisation, where the loyalty of specific parts of the population was bought with the promise of financial support and resource distribution.[1] These attempts at monopolising public life were an inheritance of Ba'athist political culture, but they may well predate actual Ba'athist rule. Ultimately, they reflect a more longstanding Leninist desire among many Iraqi parties to have state and society coincide, especially through the institutions of a party that is depicted as the vanguard of the social order to be developed. Even following a possible regime change in Baghdad, it will take a long time, and a concerted effort, to weaken this political culture.

In short, the election of a parliament has thus far hardly led to the development of a genuine political pluralism in the region. Instead, two (or, at the time of Islamic Movement rule over Halabja, three) effectively one-party statelets were formed, which are at times disparagingly referred to as 'Barzanistan' and 'Talabanistan'. Here, political opposition is tolerated in the form of small junior parties, but neither the KDP nor the PUK has tolerated activities of its main rival on the territory it considers its own. Except for the Islamic League, which captured some 20% of the vote in the latest regional elections in both KDP and PUK territory, there are hardly any substantial political alternatives to the PUK and the KDP.

The only numerically important institutions of civil society that did not depend on the local political parties appear to have been some of the Islamist organisations that rose to prominence in the 1990s. Other organisations, like the Union of the Unemployed or the various Turcoman organisations appeared to be, respectively, too weak and too dependent on foreign interference to make a lasting impression. In any case, many of these civil society institutions were almost as much institutions of patronage, distributing resources in return for loyalty, as the KDP and PUK.

But, although there is no independent civil society, a system of checks and balances has nonetheless evolved. Because the

Kurdish parties in power know that there are local alternatives, they realise that they cannot entirely ignore the population's plight and desires. In this respect, I would suggest, that the situation in the territory held by the Baghdad government is rather worse: few if any credible alternatives to the Iraqi regime have emerged, and state propaganda can conveniently blame all the shortcomings and abuses of the regime on the effects of international sanctions. In an optimistic scenario, the system of checks and balances in Iraqi Kurdistan will endure beyond the recent reconvening of the joint KDP-PUK parliament, and possibly even a change of regime in Baghdad. In an equally optimistic scenario for Iraq as a whole, one can envisage that no new administration will achieve the same concentration of power as the Ba'ath party, and that the different social forces in the country may end up striking a balance that will restrict the exercise of governmental power rather than descending into violent conflict.

Islam

Islamist organisations in the region have generally received a rather bad press, especially from sources close to, or sympathetic towards, the KDP and PUK, both largely secular nationalist Kurdish parties. But these groups, more than any other movement, have become a force to be reckoned with. They are an important voice of civil society, a voice distinct from that of the political power elite. Originating from the Iraqi branch of the Muslim Brotherhood, and partly sponsored by the international network of this organisation, it is organisations such as the Rabitay Islami or the Muslim League that have taken over the tasks of social welfare that were given up by the retreating Iraqi state and have not been fully taken over by either the Kurdish administration or by the international humanitarian effort in the region. In government-held Iraq, the Muslim Brotherhood has equally increased its presence and activities in the cities, but this seems to have happened largely with the connivance of the regime.

In all likelihood, it is such peaceful urban organisations rather than the small radical splinter groups that will remain an influential and enduring force in the region.

The recent reports about small and violent Islamist groups have tended to distract attention from the more peaceful forces that are a more important – if less visible – societal factor. Claims about links between these groups, notably Jund/Ansar, with on one hand the Iraqi regime and on the other the al-Qaeda network, have often been repeated but rarely substantiated. The number of Afghan veterans in the region has undoubtedly increased since the US-led operation in Afghanistan, but this increase seems indicative of the disintegration of the (already diffuse and personalised) Taliban/al-Qaeda network, rather than of any global Islamist master plan. Given their location, outside Iraqi-controlled territory and near the Iranian border, these small groups are also much more likely to receive support from Iran than from Baghdad. Moreover, this Iranian support is not a world-political strategy, but purely a regional trump card with which to exert pressure on the other Kurdish parties. In short: politically, radical Islam is (or has become) rather less significant than it is often made to appear; but socially, a more moderate form of political Islam is likely to remain a significant factor of life in the region for the foreseeable future.

Violence

Another social problem that emerged, or rose to prominence, in the 1990s was the increase of violence, not only between the main Kurdish parties, but also among Iraqi Kurdish society at large. The internecine fights that raged between, most importantly, the KDP, PUK and the Islamic Movement between December 1993 and October 1998 not only lost the Iraqi Kurds a good deal of the international credit and support they had acquired in the preceding years, but, locally, also led to serious social, economic, and human loss.

On another level, disturbing reports about an increase in domestic violence, especially against women, have emerged. Human rights organisations have provided credible evidence that since 1991, hundreds if not thousands of women have become victims of so-called honour killings.[2] The parties in power have been rather slow to act against these crimes. Oft-heard disclaimers that honour killings are leftovers from an allegedly traditional Islamic or tribal mentality cannot hide the fact that in scale, scope, and tactics, this violence is largely a novel phenomenon. It is at least in part a consequence of the social, economic, and political dislocations of the past decades, though it obviously cannot be justified by them. Intensive pressure from Kurdish women's groups abroad has led to both the KDP and the PUK administrations taking measures against honour killings. It remains to be seen whether these measures will lead to any substantial improvement.

Apart from these honour killings, other violent acts of a more political nature have been carried out, notably assaults against women and ladies' hairdressers. Although these have not been claimed, most of them seem to have been carried out by some of the more radical Islamist splinter groups. But on the whole, assassinations are not as numerous as during the height of instability in the mid-1990s. Moreover, public security in the Kurdish-held north at present seems to be nowhere near as bad as in government-held territory; there are consistent reports of a much more serious breakdown in law and order in Baghdad. The Iraqi government has not given up on the central tasks of its apparatus of security and repression, but apparently, it has been rather less eager to keep the ordinary policing tasks on its agenda.

The general pattern would seem to be that contemporary Iraqi Kurdistan is a rather more violent society than it was ten years ago; or at least, violence in both its domestic and public manifestations is a much more visible phenomenon. I would argue, then, that (here and in Iraq at large) the perception that violence is a legitimate means of pursuing social and/or political aims is a second long-term inheritance of more than two decades of Ba'athist rule, and one that will be difficult to eradicate. One prerequisite for such eradication is a strong and self-confident civil administration.

Economy: debt and reform

The question of whether ten years of political separation from Baghdad has caused the economy of Iraqi Kurdistan to develop characteristics qualitatively different from Iraq is rather difficult to answer. The Kurdish leadership has been reluctant to take any steps that might have led to a more radical rupture from the Iraqi economy. Thus, plans to introduce the Turkish Lira as the main local currency were hotly discussed, but ultimately rejected, in the spring of 1993. Nonetheless, the region has enjoyed a partial monetary independence since 1991, in so far as the Kurdish region continued to rely primarily on the older 'Swiss print' Iraqi Dinars, whereas in government-held territory new, locally printed banknotes became the main legal tender.

Apart from enduring social characteristics, then, long-term economic developments may crucially affect the future course of Iraq. It has been observed that authoritarian regimes can rarely master economic crises; this observation by and large applies to the Iraqi regime as well, but it should be added that the Baghdad government has had considerable success in blaming others for the consequences of its own economic policies. Thus, the regime initiated a very rapid and drastic economic privatisation drive in the late 1980s, but the harsh effects of this shock therapy have been masked by the imposition of, in 1990, UN sanctions.[3] Since then, it has been a standard (and increasingly successful) item of Iraqi propaganda to blame the sanctions for the population's suffering; but standards of living had already dropped very considerably preceding the 1990 Kuwait invasion, and were bound to fall further as a result of the government's shock therapy.

The effect of the sanctions has been, among others, to mask the continuation of policies that, for want of a better term, may be called 'neoliberal'. The state has withdrawn from most areas except for security, and private individuals close to the regime have been able to exploit, and even exacerbate, the population's plight in order to enrich themselves. The long-term consequences of Iraq's disastrous policies are, among others, the destruction of productive industrial and agricultural sectors; the radical impoverishment of the middle class sections that used to depend on the state; massive flight of people and capital; and, last but not least, a foreign debt of over US$100 billion, comparable only to that of near-bankrupt countries such as Argentina and Brazil. Much will depend on whether the existing (and largely bilateral) debts of Iraq can be successfully renegotiated rather than having a future Iraq placed under the monetary control of the IMF and the World Bank. These political and economic macrofactors have also, though perhaps not quite to the same extent, affected the Kurdish region, and they are likely to keep on doing so.

The Kurdish north had little industry to begin with; and during the 1990s, it appears to have undergone a number of parallel economic developments comparable to those in government-held areas. Thus, the withdrawal of all government personnel and the imposition of an internal blockade on the north by Baghdad in October 1991 may be seen as the most drastic form of withdrawal of the state-driven economy yet in Iraq. In its place came more 'privatised' local agencies, which were often related to the new power elites. Thus, it is widely known that many of the local NGOs that were active in the region in the early 1990s were largely front organisations for the main political parties. Following the implementation of the 1996 Food For Oil agreement between Iraq and the UN, these NGOs had little trouble in converting to contracting agencies.[4] In a way, then, in Iraqi Kurdistan and elsewhere in the country, the contracting system that was in place for much of the 1970s and 1980s appears to have been restored, albeit with a different pay master this time around: the United Nations. The constant factor in all this, of course, has been the unchanging dependence of all these systems on Iraqi oil income.

Elites and emigration

The emergence of new elites has been a largely smooth and trouble-free process due to the older economic elite, associated with the Ba'ath party, either fleeing to Baghdad or abroad, switching sides or acquiescing to the new political reality. Since the state's withdrawal in October 1991, and especially since the implementation of the lucrative Food for Oil agreement, there has been a marked increase in economic inequality. Despite the novel affluence the region has enjoyed, some 50% of the population has to survive on the equivalent of $25 per month. The Oil for Food programme provides significant relief for these destitute households, but its future is uncertain, given the volatile economic and political situation. At the same time, numerous shopping malls, amusement parks, not to mention luxurious houses, have been constructed for the newly rich. This ostentatious display of wealth has undoubtedly created resentment (which is partly articulated in Islamist terms), but at present, there are few signs that this resentment can be turned into the massive mobilisation of the poorer strata.

One dramatic social phenomenon of the past decade has been the mass emigration from the region, which at times ran at the rate of hundreds of people per week. This massive brain drain is almost certain to have very negative long-term social consequences, as it is typically younger members from the better-educated urban classes that decide to leave. The exodus of the educated middle class has been even worse in government-held territory. The Kurdish parties have done little to end this tragedy; apparently, the financial interests involved in the lucrative trade in asylum seekers outweighed their long-term social policies. However, there are some more positive sides to this brain drain, too: first, many families receive financial support from relatives abroad; and second, this international traffic has certainly increased the openness of the region. Under the Ba'ath (and especially prior to 1991), Iraq was almost hermetically sealed off; at present, there is a steady flow of people, resources and ideas to and from the region.

One factor that may in the long run benefit the further growth of civil society is the steady spread of internet facilities in the region. Recently, internet services were introduced that allow those who have a telephone connection to go online at the cost of local telephone calls; with all the information available on the web, such facilities may considerably improve the flow of ideas and discussions between the region and the rest of the world. Nevertheless, they are restricted to the relatively small percentage of households that can afford not just a telephone but also a computer, or to that part of the literate and educated youth that can afford a visit to one of the numerous internet cafés in the cities. In this respect, increased access to cyberspace does not carry much of a promise to reduce the gap between rich and poor; on the contrary, it only threatens to widen it.

Conclusion

Conventional political wisdom has it that economic liberalisation will in itself lead to democratisation, but this certainly does not apply in the case of Iraq. The privatisations that started in the 1980s have not led to the creation of a middle class that is both economically powerful and politically independent from the state; on the contrary, a 'crony capitalism' of a kind not dissimilar to that found in contemporary Egypt has emerged, with a narrow and partly new elite of party members, or even close relatives of those in power, being the prime beneficiaries of the economic restructuring.

Regarding societal developments, there appears to be some truth in the optimistic claim made by some Kurdish leaders that 'the genie is out of the bottle': it is rather unlikely that the Kurds will settle for anything less than federation, or at the very least substantial autonomy, in a future Iraq. It is also unlikely that the population would put up with a renewed extensive presence of the Iraqi security apparatus, let alone a military occupation, with which Turkey has repeatedly threatened.

Some developments, like Kurdish-language education, broadcasting and publishing, will not easily be given up. A whole generation of Kurdish youth has grown up, and to a large extent been educated, with little or no knowledge of the Arabic language and of Iraqi society and politics. This new cultural and social self-confidence will almost certainly be an enduring phenomenon. Likewise, people have for a decade not merely experienced a Kurdish voice, but a true plurality of voices in television and radio broadcasting, and through increased access to the internet. It would take a very repressive administration indeed to revert this trend towards greater Kurdish cultural and social autonomy; but this development should not be confused with either economic or political independence. The region is wholly bound to the export of Iraqi oil both under UN supervision and illegally, and to the (now privatised) welfare state system. Kurdish leaders have never expressed any substantial vision of what an independent state might look like, let alone taking action to build one.

To conclude: at present, both Iraqi Kurdistan and Iraq at large display an uneasy combination of a neoliberal economy, in which responsibility for a large part of the welfare of the population is delegated to the international humanitarian network, and a Leninist state tradition, in which those in power try (but do not necessarily manage) to monopolise civil society. Both factors would seem to impose serious structural and long-term constraints on any future process of democratisation, accompanied as they are by, on the one hand, a steady depolitisation among the population at large, and on the other an increasing concern for morality in the public sphere, as witnessed by the rise of various Islamist organisations. A reason for moderate optimism, however, may be the fact that in Iraqi Kurdistan at least, there are several major political parties around. Although none of these can be considered a full-blooded democratic organisation, they realise that they do not have a military option to use against one another, and that the very presence of a political alternative forces them to moderate their behaviour. The fact that political power is not concentrated in the hands of a single small elite as in government-held territory, but divided among competing parties pursuing their partly diverging interests, may in the longer run preclude the re-emergence of the highly centralised state like the one that dominated Iraq in preceding decades. The differences between the most important political parties and factions may not coincide with the existing social, ethnic and religious fault lines, but they do seem to carry the germ of a future Iraq that is characterised by a genuine political pluralism. But whether this relatively optimistic scenario will become a reality for Iraqi Kurdistan, let alone for Iraq as a whole, depends on factors that ultimately are largely beyond the control of local actors.

Notes

[1] For the emergence of these new forms of party clientelisation, and for the struggle between the elected structures and the politbureaus, cf. M. Leezenberg (1997) Irakisch-Kurdistan seit dem 2. Golfkrieg, In C. Borck a.o. (eds.), *Kurdologie*, Band 1. Münster: LIT Verlag.

[2] For extensive documentation, see the Kurdish Women against Honour Killing web site http://www.kurdmedia.com/kwahk/.

[3] For the market reforms, see Kiren Aziz Chaudhry, 'On the Way to the Market: Economic liberalisation and the Iraqi invasion of Kuwait', *Middle East Report* Vol 21, 1991.

[4] For an analysis of the effects of humanitarian aid, cf. M. Leezenberg, 'Humanitarian Aid in Iraqi Kurdistan' *CEMOTI*, No. 29, January-June 2000 (also available online as http://www.ceri-sciencespo.com/publica/cemoti/textes29/leezenbe.pdf)

Chapter 9

Clerics, Tribes, Ideologues and Urban Dwellers in the South of Iraq: the Potential for Rebellion

Faleh A. Jabar

As the US strategy towards Iraq shifts from containment to regime change, much will depend on the possibilities of a military mutiny and civil insurrection in Iraq itself. The memories of the 1991 uprisings are still very much alive within government and society, most notably in the southern provinces, which will play crucial roles in any future war. The 1991 uprisings that engulfed both the southern and northern provinces involved an array of social and institutional forces that far surpass the oversimplified notion of a southern Shi'ite revolt versus northern Kurdish insurrection.

While the Shia undoubtedly form the majority of the population in the southern provinces, it should be remembered that there are mixed Shia–Sunni cities, like Basra and Nassiriya. In addition, Shia themselves do not form a monolithic block. The very term, Shi'ism or Shia, has been misleadingly interpreted to denote a compact mass, a generalised social configuration imbued with union of purpose and common political motivation. The Shi'ite south of Iraq presents a much more complex picture than current perceptions among those who study Iraq would suggest.

The aim of this paper is to define and then analyse the characteristics and limitations of major social forces in the south of Iraq. These forces played a crucial role in the 1991 uprising and may well become actively engaged in the developments that would precede or follow the demise of the Ba'ath regime. In general terms, these forces are the Islamic Shi'ite movements, the Shia clerical class and tribal organisations. For the sake of brevity, the urban middle and upper classes will only be discussed in general, quantitative terms and on a nationwide basis. As with any discussion of Iraqi society, it is essential to begin with an examination of the essence of the terms Shi'ism and Shia.

Refinement of terminology

'Shi'ism' and 'Shia' are neither sociological nor political classifications, or even exact cultural terms. Apart from the fact that Shi'ism is a religious–cultural self-designation whose function is to distinguish a set of Islamic beliefs of one school from other schools, the term has no other meaningful significance. Yet, different academic approaches to Shi'ism have been plagued by a sociological reductionism.

This is especially the case in Iraq, where there is an absence of a strongly instituted Shi'ite identity. Different Shi'ite classes, the clerical class, landlord sheikhs, the political class under the monarchy from 1920 to 1958, the mercantile class, the modern middle classes, and the working and peasant classes, had different life-styles and with them different value systems, economic interests and political orientations. Primordial and modern social configurations were palpably stronger than pan-Shi'ite bonds, although a general sense of being Shi'ite always existed. One indication of the absence of a unified Shi'ite identity is that even in their religious culture, different Shi'ite groupings had different forms of religiosity. Popular ceremonial ritualism differed radically from the legalist–ethical theology of the clerical class, or from the ideologised Islamism of middle-class groups. These forms also differed from the religious piety of tribal groups in rural areas, which had a disdain for ceremonialism as 'unmanly'.

Iraqi Shi'ism also radically differs from Iranian Shi'ism. Shi'ism in Iraq is blended with Arab Bedouin culture and values. In Iran, Shi'ism has Sufi overtones and is integrated with Persian – or Iranian – nationalism. Other contrasts do exist and will be discussed later. Essentially, as Shi'ite culture took root in different national frameworks, it gave birth to varied forms, common theological tenets notwithstanding.

There are three distinct approaches that underpin academic conceptions of Shi'ism and Shia Islamist activism in Iraq: communal approaches; cultural–essentialist understandings; and conjunctural approaches. The basic tenets of the communal approach revolve around a community-versus-society dichotomy: a Sunni-minority-dominated state versus the Shi'ite-majority-oppressed community. Islamist militancy among the Shia is hence seen as an expression of grievances arising from this tense dichotomy to the exclusion of all else.

Many authors subscribe to or share some aspects of this approach. In most cases, Shi'ism, the Shia and Shi'ite Islamism figure almost as one and the same category of analysis. The Shia or Shi'ism are treated as a sociological category, a homogenous monolithic socio-cultural entity. Religious culture, in and for itself, is understood to create a unifying social and political space. This approach overlooks the social and cultural diversity within the Shia population during the agrarian epoch, the modern epoch or the transformative phase from the one to the other. Religious culture, to use Victor Turner's[1] term, forms a 'multivocal' space. The fact that forms of religiosity, as Weber[2] argued, differ widely among different social groups, has been blurred or ignored by scholars of Iraqi Shi'ism.

As distinct from the communal approach, a culturalist approach has been, more often than not, recurrently applied after the 1979 Islamic Revolution in Iran, in an attempt to explain the militancy of Islam in general and Shia Islamic radicalism in particular. Cultural essentialism attributes the rise of Islamism to the resilience of the religion as the dominant socio-historic reference for the whole of the Middle East. This notion derives from Orientalist traditions as well as from Weber's Orient–Occident cultural polarity. Incompatibility with modernity or the lack of sufficient separation between the secular and the sacred is thought to plague Islam. A variety on this approach is the notion that Shi'ism is inherently a radically anti-modern and anti-state doctrine. The Shi'ite concept of the hidden Imam, which denies legitimacy to worldly powers, is claimed to be the source of this cultural rejection of modernity. The ruling elites of the Middle East are also blamed for having allegedly succumbed to this rejectionism. In addition Shi'ism is held to be radical by dint of the logical structure of the theo-jurisitic doctrine itself; its social and political activism. This understanding of Shi'ite radicalism is asserted with no consideration of socio-political, economic or other factors. Both communal and cultural approaches share common reductionist grounds.

A subtler, conjunctional approach has provided for the comparative study of Shi'ite social movements. Hanna Batatu's[3] and the Slugletts'[4] work stand out from other research into Shi'ism and the dynamics of social change and Shia militancy in Iraq. Batatu carries sociological analyses far beyond the over-simplified culturalist and communal approaches. In the words of the Slugletts':

The notion of the heterogeneity of Iraqi society is another theme that needs further definition and refinement. The facts are that the population of Iraq ... is divided on both ethnic and sectarian lines. Of course, neither the communities nor the sects constitute homogeneous or monolithic single entities. ... A simplistic image of Iraqi society has emerged, largely under the influence of Middle Eastern 'experts' of the US defence establishment, of 'their Arab Sunnis' supporting the 'Sunni' regime of Saddam Hussein and the allegedly 'somewhat less Arab' Shia (a sort of Iranian fifth column) bitterly opposed to it.[5]

The Shi'ite Islamic movements: strengths and weaknesses

Iraqi Shi'ite Islamic movements, which contained several currents and organisations, emerged successively in the aftermath of the demise of the monarchy in 1958. The Da'wa Islamiya Party (Islamic Call) was formed in 1959, the Munazamat al-Amal al-Islami (Islamic Action Organisation) in the early 1970s and the Supreme Council of the Islamic Revolution (SCIRI) in 1982.

The Da'wa Party were the first group to emerge as a potent political force. Its development mirrored a more general fundamentalist model, one characterised by an essential culturalism married to a universal form of Islamic discourse. This led, in the first instance, to the Da'wa not developing a communitarian or sectarian ideology, but instead concentrating on the universal overtones of its rhetoric. Its main thrust was to defend the creed, Islam, in the face of creeping secularisation. The threat of secularism was acutely felt by the clerical class based in Najaf and Kazimiya. The Sunni conservative and traditionalist groups of the Muslim Brothers and the Tahrir Party shared this general approach and common enemy. The socio-economic dynamics that caused this Islamist response had been developing for decades, but they were accentuated by the radical changes instituted by the post-monarchy, military regime that seized power in 1958. The break up of landlordism, the reform of family law and the rise of the communist movement in Iraq powerfully symbolised the relative decline of religion.

The Shi'ite actors threatened by these dynamics developed two responses: a pedagogical trend by the senior, conservative members of the *ulama* (scholarly class); and an ideo-political trend developed by both the junior *ulama* and members of the Najafi mercantile and ritual-leading groups. This project of religious renewal declined as soon as the direct threat of communism waned and an accommodation contrived with changing social realities.

The second phase of the Shi'ite Islamic movement began under the authoritarian regime of the Arif brothers from 1963 until its overthrow in 1968. In an attempt to combat what it saw as the betrayal of communal distinctions, the Shi'ite movement focused on the politics of local group protests against discrimination. It shifted to a new model of communal particularism. It was during this period that Munazamat al-Amal al-Islami, headed by Ayatollah Muhamad Taqi al-Mudarissi, built the foundations to a movement that was to mature under the secular reign of the Ba'ath. While the Da'wa's origins was in Najaf, the Munazamat's following originated in Karbala. This highlights the city solidarities that underpinned and divided the growth of the Shi'ite Islamist movement.

The third phase of radicalisation came during Ba'athist rule. It was driven by the impact of the 1979 Iranian Revolution, which itself was the culmination of a radical change in political culture across the Middle East, heralded by the rise of a populist Islamism. Under the influence of the Iranian revolution, Shia militancy became over-radicalised. A premature confrontation with the Ba'ath regime in the late 1970s led to the destruction of the movement and the execution of its outstanding activists. Its spiritual leader, Muhamad Baqir al-Sadr was executed together with his sister, Bint al-Huda, in May 1980. This caused the movement's disintegration. The exodus of a large percentage of its membership led to the group being reorganised in exile in Tehran. Paradoxically, this flight helped them to mature in political and organisational terms, but cut them off from the base of their support in Iraq. As the Iraq–Iran war erupted, they joined the Iranian war effort, claiming it to be part of their sacred calling.

The Supreme Council of the Islamic Revolution (SCIRI) emerged in 1982 as the result of Iranian government efforts to unite the disparate Iraqi, mainly Shia, Islamic groups and influential individuals. Placing an Iraqi Arab at the helm, the Iranians constructed SCIRI as an umbrella organisation that included the Da'wa, the Munazamat and some Kurdish and Turkoman Islamic groups. In form, structure and intent, SCIRI resembled the later US-backed Iraqi National Congress. It was composed of independent movements who had their own manpower and resources, and who could withdraw when they wished. SCIRI's leader, Muhammad Baqir al-Hakim had his own extensive network of kin and followers outside SCIRI. A third component of the new organisation was the Badr army. However, from the outset the Badr army was placed under the full control of the Iranian government. Al-Hakim could not even visit 'his' Badr corps without permission from the Pasdaran (Iranian Revolutionary Guard). In fact, SCIRI never managed to enjoy recognition by other Shi'ite Islamic groups as their genuine representative, let alone other secular Shi'ite groups. At present, SCIRI is acting in this imagined capacity as an all-Shia spokesman and is impeding any genuine representation of secular Shi'ite forces. Its inclusion in the Washington-sponsored six opposition groups was a grave mistake indeed.

During the 1980–88 Iran–Iraq war, the movement as a whole pinned its hopes on an Iranian military success to remove Saddam Hussein. In doing this it underestimated the strength of Iraqi nationalism as a unifying ideology that managed to override or, at least, paper over communal distinctions.

The growth of the Shi'ite Islamic movement in Iraq has been undermined by its inherent socio-political weaknesses. Firstly, Shi'ite Islamic activism could not count on the clerical class, which is numerically small, has weak networks of influence, and limited financial resources from *khums* (religious taxes) and other revenues. The conservative (non-activist) sections of the clerical class opposed the formation of an Islamic party along modern lines because it contradicted their interpretation of the tenets and structure of religious authority. These are based on the idea that authority runs from God to the Prophet, then on to the *imams*[6] and finally down to the *mujtahids*.[7] The latter felt that the formation of an Islamic party would compete with the religious class and their God-given authority.

Secondly, in comparison to Iran, Shi'ite religious rituals in Iraq, as cultural spaces of Shi'ite identity and instruments of mass mobilisation and agitation, are sparse, segmented and fragmented. Mainly based in city quarters, they are characterised by weak social networks and dominated by traditional families. Only in Najaf and Karbala are these rituals embedded in the local *hay'at* (socio-economic bodies), the remnants of old artisan guilds. This social basis to rituals in Najaf provided the leadership for the anti-Ba'ath agitation in 1977. However, that was the first and so far the last contribution of leadership made by the *hay'at* organisations.

The Da'wa Islamic Party, tried to act as a bridge uniting both the *marja* (figures of religious authority) and social spaces created by religious ritual. But the Da'wa never managed to control these two social dynamics, which retained much of their autonomy. By contrast, the Iranian revolution could rely on clerical networks and the ritual spaces as instruments of mobilisation and recruitment. Without this organisational base within society, the Iraqi case called for a modern, centralised political party to provide structure and direction to political protest. The clerical class inhibited the creation and development of such a modern organisation. Nowhere has the weakness of these three circles of Shi'ite activism been clearer than under the Ba'ath regime. The supreme *marja*, Sayyid Muhsin al-Hakim (who died in 1970), the ritual leaders and the Da'wa failed in their successive challenges to the Ba'ath between 1970 and 1974.

The two social groups that initiated the Shi'ite Islamic movement in Iraq, the junior generation of clerics in Najaf and Karbala, together with the traditional Najafi middle and petty merchants in late 1950s, had different orientations and aims. The clerics set about creating a mobilising ideology, while the merchants focused on action and organisation. With the flow of disadvantaged and disfranchised middle- and lower-class migrant Shia into Baghdad and major cities during the 1970s and 1980s, the movement changed its social composition. It now contained wide sections of the Shi'ite lower and middle classes, along with poor migrant Shia groups recently arrived from the countryside. The educated elements recognised the need for a coherent leadership and competed with the clerics for this role. A generational, social and ideological rift soon evolved out of these differences and rivalries. Paradoxically, the supremacy of the clerics was only preserved by the application of Iranian pressure.

One of the crucial paradoxes in the development of these groupings was that as they matured as modern social movements, with disciplined organisation and clear-cut political programmes, they were severed from their national habitat and thrown into exile. From there they were quickly integrated into the Iranian war effort against Iraq.

Until 1988, the Shia movement in exile conceived the war as the only way to achieve power in Iraq. A consequence of this political position was that while Iranian Shi'ite activism appeared as a distinctly national movement with a peripheral Islamic internationalist interest, the Iraqi Shia Islamic groups appeared as an internationalist movement with a peripheral national interest. This reality isolated the Shia movement from the mainstream Iraqi patriotism that emerged during the Gulf War and was embraced by the majority of the Shia who fought Iran. When the Iranian war effort came to a halt, the Iraqi Shi'ite Islamic movements lost direction and started to fracture. The previous, social and regional divisions deepened and resulted in a series of splits driven by ideological, political, ethnic, national, local and even familial factors. It was during this post-1988 period that migration to the West for asylum reached its peak.

The 1991 Gulf War offered the Islamic movement (the Da'wa, Munazamat and SCIRI) both an opportunity for mobilisation within Iraq, but also a test of their strength and coherence. The scattered local uprisings in a host of southern Shia cities and townships were triggered by the retreating, humiliated men of the Iraqi army, indignant local Ba'athi officials, tribal groups and society at large. Crossing the porous southern border between Iran and Iraq, SCIRI and the Da'wa managed to deploy a few hundred armed militants. But after this deployment they failed to lend the scattered mutinies a command-and-control system, or to offer any sense of spiritual leadership. The rebels in southern Iraq instead referred themselves to the highest religious authority in Najaf, the Ayatollah al-Uzma, Abul Qasim al-Khoi. SCIRI's lack of leadership was exacerbated when their fighters brought with them the disastrous slogans of the Iranian Islamic revolution with their accompanying sectarian overtones. They carried large photographs of Khomeini, unwittingly alienating the retreating military and other secular-minded or non-sectarian rebels. Weakened by further splits in the aftermath of the 1991 rebellions, SCIRI, Da'wa and Munazamat may not be able to improve their performance during any possible US-led attempt at regime change in Iraq.

Institutionalised religion: the clerical class in Iraq

The clerical class in Najaf is the source of the highest religious authority in Iraq. Unlike secular organisations, no Shia movement based on theology can ever override the authority of this supreme jurisprudent. Khomeini bypassed the chain of legitimacy in Shi'ite jurisprudence by using his capacity as a *marja* (a religious authority) rather than as a leader of an Islamic party.

High-ranking *mujtahids* derive their authority from a variety of sources: knowledge of the sacred; a network of disciples and vast numbers of lay-emulators; and the size of religious taxes accruing to them. State patronage may also be instrumental in this regard. Historically, the Shi'ite clerical class in Iraq has been very weak compared to its Iranian counterpart. The latter built a strong financial basis to its influence and developed popular urban constituencies organised around the old guild and guild-like movements. It could also rely on a rich religious calendar punctuated with numerous rituals. An added source of strength was the fact that Iranian Shi'ism was successfully blended with Persian nationalism.

By contrast, the Iraqi clerical class was very weak. This class was divided by lineage, city and ethnicity. The fractured nature of the institution of *marja'ism* (religious authority) has long been a decisive feature accounting for this weakness. This accentuated the theological, ideological and political divisions between the towns of Karbala, Najaf and Kazimiya, and between Persian and Arab elements, and finally between influential notable families. The clerical class also lacked solid social alliances with the Shi'ite social classes based on property and capital, or with middle-class intellectuals.

Even when there was a limited alliance between high clerics and the modern Shia movements, the effect was not altogether positive. The supportive part of the clerical class brought to the movement their social networks of emulators, their financial power (however limited) as collectors of religious taxes (*khums*) and, most importantly, their legitimisation as holders of religious symbols and beliefs. But this class also brought to the movement dynamics that inhibited its ability to mobilise the population. Firstly, the religious class was organised along primordial sub-national lines and this brought divisions to the Shia movement organised within the national unit of Iraq. Secondly, the clerical class is also organised in traditional supra-national networks of emulators and agents (*wukala*). This mode of traditional organisation collided with the political need for nationally defined politics. Thirdly, clerical authority competed with party politics as rival centres of power, creating an antagonistic duality focusing on who should command the submission of lay society. Fourthly, the clerical class dominated the production of ideology and delayed the secular drive for the renewal and updating of the movement's demands. Finally, this class also monopolised leadership posts and decision-making in the emerging modern organisations, hindering the upward political mobility of a new generation of educated, active lay Shia. This was paradoxical, since numerically and in terms of influence, the clerical class was declining as the new, modern middle classes were growing. The powerful positions that the clerical class held did not reflect the actual power relations between these two sections of the movement. Inside Shia movements, the supremacy of the clerical class was artificially maintained by the demands of the Iranian clerics. In society at large, however, such prominence gradually gained momentum in the aftermath of the 1991 defeat for quite different reasons.

In the wake of the 1991 rebellion, the government in Baghdad set about destroying those civil associations and institutions that had managed to survive under Ba'ath rule. The ensuing social vacuum was filled by the religious networks and charitable services that some leading clerics had managed to assemble. War, dislocation and fear of the numerous uncertainties in their lives drove ordinary Shia towards their spiritual leaders. One indication of this phenomenon is the staggering growth in pilgrimage to the Shi'ite holy shrines. According to official figures, more than two million pilgrims (almost

10% of the total population, and around 20% of the Shi'ite population) travelled to Karbala to commemorate the martyrdom of Imam Hussein in 1999. In 2001, the figure reached 2.4 million. These figures should be read against the background of the activism of the late Ayatollah Muhammad Sadiq al-Sadr, who was assassinated together with his two elder sons in Najaf in 1999.

Al-Sadr was originally a handpicked government appointee, but he grew publicly critical of Ba'ath party rule in his widely attended sermons. For the first time in a generation, a Shi'ite *imam* built vast networks of followers among the peasantry and the urban middle classes, and forged an alliance with influential urban merchants and tribal chieftains. Since 1990, urban merchants and tribal leaders have gained relative social power from the acute economic polarisation that has accompanied ten years of war and sanctions.

Sadr's extended family, along with other leading Najaf and Karbala families, will again undoubtedly supply new leaders of prominence. The Khoi group, which relies on the apolitical Ayatollah Sistani, based in Najaf, will play a crucial role in this process. Such new centres of religious authority, born in the period since 1990, may well surpass the influence of any or all Shi'ite Islamic groups working against the Ba'ath from Iranian exile.

Tribalism, a powerful new social force

The rise in influence of Sayyids (noble descendants of Imam Ali) and *mujtahids* was part of a general social and cultural change that has characterised Iraq society in the 1990s. Among a number of the rising status groups, tribal sheikhs (chieftains) hold a key position. The political influence and social power of tribes in Iraq has been steadily declining since the Ottoman economic and political reform of the late nineteenth century. Ottoman Iraq was notoriously known among tribesmen as the 'graveyard of the tribes'. Tribes thrived where no central power competed for influence or dominated them. After the centralisation of Ottoman power across the Empire, Arabia became their safe haven.

The course of tribal disintegration appeared lineal and was steady. Large tribal confederations, like the Muntafiq in the south, began to break up into segments. Sheikhs became absentee landlords and tribesmen became landless or sharecropping peasants. A centralised government took over various tribal functions, from the administration of justice to settling land and water disputes, the registration of land, education and law and order. Migration, modern education, the commercialisation of the peasant economy and strong government administration reduced tribal cohesion even further. In the majority of cases, tribes were reduced to small extended families, village communities, or surnames with historical resonance. The residues of old social organisations managed to keep their own value system, lifestyle and kinship ideology in rural areas and small provincial towns.

Successive blows weakened tribal landlords. Agrarian reforms stripped them of their economic power-base, and with the destruction of the monarchy in 1958, eliminated their political influence. The steady decline in tribal influence was the order of things until 1970. However, the seizure of power by the Ba'ath transformed tribal fortunes. Various forms of tribalism were constructed, encouraged or manipulated by the state.

First, *étatist* or political tribalism was constructed. This was a process of integrating Saddam Hussein's own tribal lineage and organisation into the state to enhance the power of a vulnerable ruling elite. Political tribalism is still functioning, but shows signs of weakness and age.

Secondly, the Ba'ath revived military tribalism. The Ba'ath regime rediscovered and exploited military tribalism among the Kurds. The tribal Aghas (or chiefs) of the Sorchy, Mezouri, Doski, Herki and Zibari tribes were recruited as mercenaries to fight against the nationalist Kurdish movement as early as 1974. Such military services became even more crucial during the Iraq–Iran war. Groups from 100,000 to 150,000 Kurds were organised in Battalions of National Defence (*Afwaj al-Difa' al-Watani*). The promotion of political and military tribalism by the Ba'ath reversed the decline of tribal chieftains and tribal ideology. In the first case, individuals were first detached from kinship groups and incorporated into state institutions. As soon as they gained power and wealth, their tribal kin benefited and thrived from their patronage. They recognised that the Ba'athi state was exploiting them; and reciprocated in kind. In the second case, Aghas favoured by the state got richer and more powerful. They were not only providers of employment for their poor fellow tribesmen or their village vassals but were also necessary mediators with state institutions. Statist tribalism was exclusive by nature, confined to the ruling class kinship networks. Military tribalism, by contrast, spread mainly, but not exclusively, among Kurdish tribes.

By contrast, the third form of tribalism – social tribalism – is a revival, manipulation or invention of tribal structures formed out of cultural kinship networks and values, existing among rural migrants or in provincial towns. During the Iraq–Iran war, the regime discovered the vitality of the Arab tribes in the south, who fought effectively against Iranian forces. They were soon collectively approached to bolster the domestic rule of the Ba'ath party.

Another feature was the rise of tribal notables in social life during the late 1980s, largely because of the decline of modern civil associations. As Ba'ath party organisation weakened, primordial networks were reinvigorated to fill a social void. This cultural tribalism was not an invention of the state, but was rather a part of the social fabric of a society in rapid and destructive transition. State intervention empowered cultural tribalism to take new roles. Encouraged by the government to take charge of law and order, old tribal families took the business seriously. This reconstruction of tribes, real or fictive, spread quickly. Ironically, the reconstructed tribes moved into urbanised, civic spaces.

This process reached its peak in 1992, when Saddam Hussein held an audience of tribal chieftains in his palace. He apologised for the agrarian reforms of the past 30 years and promised reconciliation. In return the tribal sheikhs hoisted their banners aloft and took an oath of allegiance to the president, reborn as the chief of chiefs. Exempted from military service, they were provided with light arms, communication and transport facilities to impose law and order in their districts.

Major tribes, mostly Sunnis, were charged with national security tasks; minor tribes took local duties such as law and order, dispute settlement and tax collection. All were encouraged to operate as an extension of state organs. The revival of the tribes as social actors stems from the need to fill the void created by the destruction of civil society institutions, and from the decline of the state itself as the provider of security and justice. These newly revived or invented tribes do not operate in their traditional habitat, the rural areas, but in urban centres, damaging the very fabric of an urbanised and cultured society.

Today tribes in the south of Iraq are not coherent social groups, but are vertically divided. One section may enthusiastically cooperate with the government while another opposes it. These vertical divisions mean that it is not possible to draw up a list of pro-regime or anti-regime tribes. Saddam Hussein has reinvigorated tribal organisations in order to strike a balance with other contending forces both within society and the state that threaten his continued rule.

But this process can easily backfire. Pro-government Kurdish tribal mercenaries took the lead in the 1991 rebellion. Their uprising was initiated by a Mezouri–Doski alliance in Dohok. Their mutiny dramatically changed power relations in the region and forced Iraqi army units in the northern sector to lay down their arms. It also paved the way for angry civilians to storm government offices. Southern Arab tribes also rebelled, but did not take a lead role in the movement. In the forthcoming confrontation, they may have a larger input. A strong alliance has been forged between key southern tribes and the clerical class in Najaf. They also have grievances against the government. This combination will provide both the moral backing and motivation for anti-regime activism.

The upper and middle classes

Social engineering under the Ba'ath targeted both traditional and modern social groups. The Ba'athist regime deployed oil wealth and the command economy to restructure, bribe and manipulate Sufi orders, and Sayyid families in addition to Kurdish, Sunni and Shia tribes. In a series of calculated steps, bizarre amalgams of business groups have also been created. A form of kinship capitalism (as opposed to crony capitalism) has been constructed. A market-based space has been formed for individuals tied to the regime through tribal, familial or patronage links. Such a policy achieved two contradictory aims: it enhanced the command economy, with the state at its pinnacle, uniting through the use of patronage the political and economic spheres; and it created a protected space for the development of a warped form of free market.

However, the evolution of this kinship capitalism did not undermine the state's control of the economy. All business associations are supervised or appointed by the government. This includes the Industrial Union, Chambers of Commerce, and the

Contractors Union. Worker's trade unions, on the other hand, have been integrated into the party's 'mass organisations'. With the merger of the Ministries of Industry and Military Production, the Iraqi work force, as a matter of course, were turned into men in uniform, liable to the norms of military discipline.

The upper business class thrived under the reign of this contradictory nationalist socialism. The millionaires of this class grew quickly from 50 or so families in 1968 to some 800 in 1980, and on to an estimated 3,000 in 1990. The Industrial League, which only had 160 members in 1960, grew to a membership of 6,000 large and medium industrialists by 1990. In the same period, the Contractors Union's membership went up from around 800 to 3,329. Official members of the Chambers of Commerce, notably those with import licences, grew to more than 10,000. An estimated 25,000 very rich families constitute roughly one in every 1,000 of the population.

Deregulation in 1987 gave a boost to this process, with the selling of selected public industrial assets also helping. Under sanctions, 'fat cats' (as they are contemptuously known in Baghdad) thrived and increased in number as they built lucrative import networks. The striking of partnerships with influential governmental or quasi-governmental figures, like Uday Hussein, the president's eldest son, is an indication of the political roots of this new entrepreneurial class.

The old business class that the Ba'ath faced when assuming power have been restructured beyond recognition. Many Shia mercantile and industrial families were deported to Iran and had their property confiscated. Only those considered loyal to the government were left intact or favoured. A select few from the Kurdish tribes loyal to the regime like the Sorchi, Herki, Mezuri and Dosky (among others), were picked to join the club of the wealthy.

The modern Iraqi middle classes had a divergent trajectory. This group, generally speaking, formed the backbone of Ba'ath support. An estimated 34% of the urban population in 1968, this stratum surpassed 50% by the end of the Iraq–Iran War. Almost doubling in 20 years, the middle class were dependent on a fragile and unsound expansion of the service economy. Reliant on oil revenues, services were at the mercy of the fluctuating oil price and production output. With the crippling effects of the massive war expenditure during the 1980s, and the bite of sanctions in the 1990s, the salaried middle classes were reduced to paupers. Their sons were the canon fodder in two devastating wars and they lost faith in the Ba'ath's official socialist-nationalism. Prospects for upward mobility via party membership had drawn large sections of this group into the Ba'ath's ideological orbit during the 1970s. As the state's largesse disappeared, they deserted the party.

A majority of the war generation rebelled in 1991; a majority of the sanctions generation may well rebel in the twenty-first century. Immersed in the values of violence and plunged into intolerable ruin and poverty, the middle classes nationwide are deeply alienated from the regime. Among the southerners this anti-regime revulsion is reinforced by official disdain and disregard for those provinces that rebelled in 1991. They are denied the meagre services that the government usually provides, and the population is treated as a community of suspects.

The modern, educated classes depend on education for their upward mobility. Deprived of property or capital, their only hope for improvement is a vibrant economy with a strong national currency, rule of law and equal opportunities for all. De-ideologised and segmented, the social groupings that make up society in southern Iraq may well act as the cutting edge of dissent, but their very segmentation may hinder their capability to form a coherent collective movement with sound leadership. Traditional chiefs and dignitaries may fill this vacuum.

Conclusion

The southern part of Iraq may well be a haven of anti-Ba'ath opposition over the next year. While Shia form the bulk of the population, there are mixed Sunni–Shia areas. Shia in general do not constitute a homogeneous community, but are structured in sundry modern classes or segmented traditional organisations like tribes, status groups and extended families.

Opposition to Ba'ath rule may have different connotations for different social groups. A mutinous, violent and de-ideologised mentality permeates the war and sanctions generations. With the inherent weakness of organised political parties that would have been expected to lend purpose and offer leadership to the scattered communities, the possible developments in the aftermath of invasion and war involve an array of potential trends, ranging from sustained, organised or disorganised rebellions to mob-like violence or gangster-like retribution. This destructive and constructive potential has a 'Jekyll and Hyde' nature. It would help bring Ba'athist rule to an end, but could also bring forth unfettered chaos.

While the younger generation may provide a rebellious and/or destabilising force, clerical dignitaries and tribal chieftains could offer a moderating element, restraining the youth and counterbalancing the Islamic parties at present based in Iran. Otherwise, the Shia ideological parties, protégés of the conservatives in the Iranian government, may introduce powerful communal dynamics into society. This could endanger the potential for a smooth transition to a post Ba'athist politics, dominated by the rule of law and an emerging democracy. The Shia middle and upper business classes may well be another moderating force bolstering the transition to democracy. These classes could supply members of representative bodies. Having commercial experience and widespread contacts within their own communities, the Shia business class can also act as a counter-balance to any rise in fundamentalism.

Notes

[1] See Victor Turner, *Dramas, fields, and metaphors: symbolic action in human society* (Cornell University Press, London, 1974); Victor Turner, *The ritual process: structure and anti-structure* (Routledge and Kegan Paul, London, 1969); and Max Weber, *The Sociology of Religion* (Methuen, London, 1965).

[2] Max Weber, *Economy and Society*, (University of California Press: LA) edited by Guenther Roth and Claus Wittich, volume 1, 1978 (1968), p399.

[3] See for example Hanna Batatu, *The Old Social Classes and the Revolutionary Movements of Iraq. A Study of Iraq's Old Landed and Commercial Classes and its Communists, Ba'thists, and Free Officers* (Princeton University Press, Princeton, New Jersey, 1989); Sami Zubaida, *Islam, the people and the state : essays on political ideas and movements in the Middle East* (I.B. Tauris, London, 1993); Juan Cole and Nikkie Keddie, *Shi'ism and social protest* (Yale University Press, New Haven, 1986); and Olivier Roy, *The failure of political Islam* (I.B.Tauris, London, 1994) among others.

[4] Marion Farouk-Sluglett and Peter Sluglett, 'The Historiography of Modern Iraq', *American History Review*, December 1991, p. 1412-3.

[5] Ibid, p. 1408-1421.

[6] Imams are sacred and infallible. There are twelve starting with Imam Ali, the cousin and son in law of Prophet Muhammad, his son Hassan, then his son Hussain. The other nine are the descendants of Hussain, the third Imam

[7] Mujtahids are doctors of religion, they are mundane and fallible. They represent the Imam who is the sole legitimate ruler of the Muslim community.